THE TAO OF YAO

Insights from Basketball's Brightest Big Man

Oliver Chin

Frog, Ltd.
Berkeley, California

Published by Frog, Ltd.

Frog, Ltd. books are distributed by
North Atlantic Books
P.O. Box 12327
Berkeley, California 94712

Cover photo © Robert Seale, for *The Sporting News*
Cover and book design by Paula Morrison

Printed in the United States of America

North Atlantic Books' publications are available through most bookstores. For further information, call 800-337-2665 or visit our website at www.northatlanticbooks.com.

Substantial discounts on bulk quantities are available to corporations, professional associations, and other organizations. For details and discount information, contact our special sales department.

Library of Congress Cataloging-in-Publication Data

Chin, Oliver Clyde, 1969–
    The tao of Yao : insights from basketball's brightest big man / by Oliver Chin.
        p. cm.
    ISBN 1-58394-090-1 (pbk.)
    1. Yao, Ming, 1980–   2. Basketball players—China—Biography.
3. Taoism.   I. Title.
    GV884.Y66C55 2003
    796.357'092—dc22

                                        200301735

1 2 3 4 5 6 7 8 9 MALLOY 09 08 07 06 05 04

THE TAO OF YAO

"Oliver Chin uses the modern phenomenon of Yao Ming to illustrate the ancient wisdom of Taoism and Sun Tzu's *The Art of War*. By deftly bridging the cultures of East and West, by drawing inspiration from sports heroes, warriors, and philosophers over thousands of years of history, *The Tao of Yao* transcends both time and space, highlighting universal principles of leadership essential to victory."

—Iris Chang, the *New York Times* bestselling author of *The Rape of Nanking* and *The Chinese in America: A Narrative History*

Table of Contents

1. The Wonder of Yao 1

2. The Meaning of the Tao......................... 19

3. The Wisdom of Lao 27

4. The Cultural Ambassador....................... 35

- *National Pride ... 36*

- *The Houston Globetrotters ... 45*

- *Coming to America ... 55*

5. The Rookie 67

- *The Bite of Charles Barkley ... 80*

6. The Art of Traveling............................ 91

- *On the Road Again 95*

- *Family Ties ... 100*

- *Local Hospitality ... 106*

7. The Aim of Athletics........................... 113

- *There Is No "I" in Team ... 125*

- *The Forgotten Fundamentals ... 132*

- *The Passing Principle ... 140*

8. Sports Are War 147

- *Enemy Mine* . . . *150*

- *The Force* . . . *153*

- *The Tao of Offense and Defense* . . . *156*

- *Shaq Attack: War of the Words—and Worlds* . . . *161*

- *Game Faces* . . . *168*

- *Stars and Stripes* . . . *173*

9. Being in the Center 181

- *The Anti-Center* . . . *187*

10. Lighting the Way 197

- *The Ming Is the Message* . . . *200*

- *The Rise of a Shooting Star* . . . *207*

Appendix: Statistics 217

Endnotes 223

Index 245

To my sisters Pamela and Brenda
and brothers Geoffrey and Randy
who taught me how to play the game.

Chapter 1

The Wonder of Yao

My words are very easy to understand and very easy to practice.
Yet no one in the world can understand them;
No one can practice them.
My words have their sources, my deeds their precedents.
If people do not understand that, they do not understand me.[1]

—Lao Tzu

The Profile on Yao

Height:	7'5"
Weight:	295 lbs
Position:	Center
Birthdate:	September 12, 1980
Birthplace:	Shanghai, China

"As the traveler who has once been from home is wiser than he who has never left his own doorstep, so a knowledge of one other culture should sharpen our ability to scrutinize more steadily, to appreciate more lovingly, our own."[2]

—Margaret Mead

It's not every day that someone can come out of nowhere and become the world's most popular athlete. Especially when you're 7 feet 5 inches tall.

But Yao Ming managed to pull it off.

Little known outside the People's Republic of China for his first twenty years of life, Yao liked it that way. Deep into the whirlwind of his first season in the National Basketball Association (NBA), he reminded a throng of reporters in a pre-game press conference in New York City: "You have to understand, I don't like to be bothered by a lot of people."[3]

However, standing head and shoulders above the crowd makes anonymity difficult. Size carries its own set of expectations. Namely, if you're tall, strangers assume that you should be good at playing basketball. Given the escalating hoopla over Yao, it provides some context to flash back a few years before he strode onto the world's center stage.

The old roundball adage is that "You can't teach height." In China the average height for men is 5'5" versus 5'8" in the US. At nine, Yao was so tall that his classmates picked him as the athlete most likely to succeed even though Yao professes, "At that time I couldn't shoot at all. I could only make a layup if no one else was around."[4] He shouldn't feel so bad. Famed for his tremendous agility at 6'9" and 220 lbs, Bill Russell was a five-time MVP and an eleven-time NBA champion. But even he suffered from having two left feet in high school: "I was clumsy at everything. When I opened a soup can, it felt as if I was trying to take apart a watch with a sledgehammer.... [After my first practice] I dropped football,

"Throw in his enormous size, and he's the most compelling NBA player since MJ in his prime, 'Ripley's Believe It or Not' crossed with Pete Newell's Big-Man Moves instructional video. When he's running the court, you can't take your eyes off Yao. I don't even feel that way about Shaq."[5]

—Bill Simmons, ESPN

swallowed my pride and went out for the cheerleading team. I didn't even make that."[6]

Yao's first coach Li Zhangming said that the young Ming was a work in progress: "He didn't like basketball very much in the beginning. He was so much taller than the other kids and an awkward mover. It took time to cultivate his interest, by playing games and making him feel the fun of basketball."[7]

As a twelve-year-old, Yao was already six and a half feet high. So it was no surprise that the teen faced a different future. In retrospect, Yao lists the immediate down sides to growing so fast: "Well, I guess I had to pay the bus fare earlier than anyone else. And the doors seemed to be getting shorter for me."[8]

Soon, at the age of fourteen, he joined the throng vying to make the local junior varsity (JV) squad of the Shanghai Sharks, a professional team financed by a state-run TV station. Tryouts were no walk in the park, but Yao did make the JV team, and later he did become a full-fledged Shark. By the time the team enrolled in another pro league sponsored by Nike, Yao was sixteen years old and almost seven feet tall. Accepted into the Shanghai Sports College, Yao finally showed up on the sports juggernaut's radar. Nike's director of marketing for China at the time, Terry Rhoads, recalled, "I first saw Yao in '97. Nike had just signed a contract to sponsor the Shanghai Sharks of the Chinese Basketball Association, and we had a little party to introduce ourselves. A few of us were there when in walked the team. Looked normal, guys 6'4". Then this one kid comes in, baby-faced, who's about 7'3", kind of skinny and in some ways looking like Manute Bol. Our jaws dropped, and then, of course, the skepticism came. Well, he's probably a stiff. But once he started hitting three-pointers, we thought—Whoa!"[9]

Evidently, Nike liked what they saw. Yao was invited to Nike's 1997 summer camp in Paris, and the next year in San Diego. Then in 1999 Nike signed Yao to a four-year endorsement contract for $200,000. Though it sounds like a lot, this sum pales in comparison with Nike's bank-busting arrangement with 18-year-old LeBron James. The #1 pick of the 2003 draft by the Cleveland Cavaliers, the 6'8" phenom skipped college altogether to seize a Midas-like payday. "King James" got a $10 million signing bonus from Nike on top of a seven-year deal for $90 million, with sales incentives that could double the total take. With outlays like these, sponsoring athletes is like placing bets on a roulette table. Most gambles don't pan out, but if you're lucky a long shot will hit the jackpot.

Yao did. Being tall is good, but being talented is better. In every year of playing in the Chinese basketball league, Yao steadily improved both his scoring and accuracy. Clearly growing comfortable within his frame, Yao later would conclude that his height definitely had at least one major benefit: "You have to understand the air I breathe is a lot fresher."[10]

Still Yao had higher to climb, as he represented China at the 2000 Summer Olympics. Traveling to Sydney, Australia, Yao suddenly faced top-flight international competition for the first time. Of course, this included the Americans from the NBA. Under the wary glare of a bevy of Western pros, coaches, and scouts, Yao succeeded in not only piquing their curiosity but also whetting their appetites. At the time the coach of Team USA, Rudy Tomjanovich, observed, "[Yao] Ming is gigantic and very young. He can have a very good future. Usually a guy who grows that fast doesn't have ball-handling skills, but he does."[11] Holding his ground commendably against all comers, Yao was no longer a well-kept secret. Even after the US improved its record in international play to a gaudy 102−2 at China's expense, Yao looked toward the future: "China is worried about losing their best players to the NBA. But the players will learn a lot in the NBA and come back and spread the knowledge. . . . I will play in the NBA, but today it is hard to say which team I will play for."[12]

One of those impressed was Bill Walton. Following in the collegiate footsteps of 7'2" Lew Alcindor (before he changed his name to Kareem Abdul-Jabbar), the 6'11" Walton extended the hallowed 88-game winning streak of UCLA's coach John Wooden. Abdul-Jabbar won two NCAA Player of the Year awards and led his teams to three national championships and an 88−2 record. Walton was NCAA Player of the Year three times and led the Bruins to two crowns and an 86−4 mark. (In 1994 UCLA would retire the numbers of both men at the 25th anniversary of their stadium Pauley Pavilion.) In 1974, the Portland Trail Blazers made Walton the #1 pick of the NBA draft. In turn he promptly pulled them out of the basement and made them an instant contender. Soon the Blazers won the title in 1977 and Walton was crowned league MVP in 1978.

However, the bright future of the "Big Redhead" was unexpectedly cut short. Hobbled by debilitating foot, ankle, and knee injuries, Walton could no longer perform up to the caliber he was accustomed to and stomached an unfamiliar stretch of mediocrity with the San Diego Clippers, a woeful expansion team. Nearing the premature end of his career, he leapt at the chance to become a supporting actor on Larry Bird's stellar Boston Celtics. It was a wise move. In his last full season, 1985–86, Walton helped the Celtics defeat the Houston Rockets and their vaunted "Twin Towers," 7'4" Ralph Sampson and Hakeem Olajuwon, and won the league's "Sixth Man" award. Limping through one more injury-plagued year, Walton retired after the Celtics lost to the Lakers in the finals. Subsequently, he was a shoe-in for the Naismith Memorial Basketball Hall of Fame in 1993.

Like many exceptional athletes before him, Walton decided that his next career would be in television. Since becoming a basketball announcer, he has cemented his preexisting reputation of being an outspoken man who follows the beat of his own drummer. After the Sydney Olympics, *ESPN The Magazine* dedicated its December 2000 cover story to exposing a "Hidden Dragon," and in it Walton duly shared his personal opinions:

The Sporting News

◄ Bill Walton posts up fellow Hall-of-Famer Dan Issel.

"You watch an old, old guy like that, with the most hammered body in sports, acting like a high school kid—it's both funny and inspiring at the same time. Every game was a challenge, and he didn't let any of us forget that."

—Kevin McHale

The Wonder of Yao

7

As we approach the halfway point of the Age of Shaq, the search for a successor has extended to the least likely of places: China. Why? If you watched the Olympics, you know. I was there, and after watching Yao Ming compete against the best players in the world, I left Sydney dizzy with the possibilities. Simply put, the 20-year-old Yao has a chance to alter the way the game of basketball is played.... This guy has skills, competitiveness and basketball intelligence that far exceed his limited background. As I watched his crisp and imaginative passes, felt the energy surge when he'd whip an outlet to launch a fast break and noted his decision-making and great court demeanor, I knew I was peering into the future.... Yes, Yao is unquestionably a work-in-progress. But if I were an NBA coach, I'd like him to be my work-in-progress. He's 7'6" and incredibly graceful and coordinated. Over the past 15 years, the NBA has put a higher premium on physical talent than on skill. The international game favors the opposite, skill without the physical prowess. Yao Ming has the chance to be the bridge that spans both worlds.[13]

Larry Brown was the first and only American man to win an Olympic gold medal as both a basketball player (as a 5'9" guard in 1964) and a coach (assisting Tomjanovich in 2000). Having taken the reins of many an NBA team, Brown would soon leave his post in Philadelphia to coach the Detroit Pistons. But seeing Yao compete firsthand in Australia, Brown concurred with Walton on Yao's potential: "In four years, he could be one of the best players in the world."[14]

THE TAO OF YAO

ﾟ

Let's fast-forward two years. The Houston Rockets had an abysmal 2001–2002 season where they lost almost twice as often as they won, compiling a heinous 28–54 record. Faced with the unenviable task of rebuilding, they had the dubious fortune of contending for the first pick in next year's draft. Nevertheless, coach Rudy Tomjanovich was still optimistic: "It hasn't been fun losing. But if there's one thing I know now, it is that good things often come from bad things. We're going to make good things come of this. I guarantee it."[15]

Tomjanovich had spent his whole career in Houston. As a 6'8" shooting forward, #45 was an All-Star five times in his eleven seasons and became the team's all-time leading scorer. Retiring on October 2, 1981, he would become the first of five Rockets to get his number retired. Chalking up nine years as an assistant, he was tapped then to be head coach and never looked back. Over the next twelve years, Rudy T became the franchise's leader in wins and winning percentage, and brought home two NBA titles to the stadium known as The Summit. But it was a humbling trek back down from the top. By 2002 the glory from the Rockets' repeat championships in 1994 and 1995 had long since faded.

But it wasn't that long ago when the Rockets had looked for a big man to reverse their fortunes. Back in 1984, they won the coin flip for the #1 draft pick and chose the Nigerian-born Hakeem Olajuwon, a local star from the University of Houston. At UH, Olajuwon was the starting center of the fast and furious fraternity of "Phi Slamma Jamma" with

Clyde "the Glide" Drexler, which had just been upset in the NCAA title game. Now Olajuwon headlined the 1984 draft, which is still considered one of the NBA's best ever: Michael Jordan was picked #3, Charles Barkley #5, and scrappy playmaker John Stockton #16. Nicknamed the "Dream," the 7-foot Olajuwon had big shoes to fill, since he followed in the wake of the tenacious 6'10", 255-lb man-mountain Moses Malone. All the same, Hakeem perfected the moves of a whirling dervish with a lethal fade-away jumpshot and pump fake, and a decade later he led the Rockets to two NBA crowns.

However, success is a fickle mistress, and pro sports exemplifies the motto "Winning isn't everything, it's the only thing." Los Angeles Lakers Magic Johnson and Kareem Abdul-Jabbar liked to quote their intense coach Pat Riley who claimed, "There are two possible states of being in the NBA—winning and misery."[16] After Olajuwon's somber departure from the Rockets in 2001 and retirement a year later (after being exiled to the lowly Toronto Raptors), Houston was firmly thrust back to square one.

Now, against all odds, the Rockets thanked their lucky stars. On May 19, 2002, they started the morning with the fifth-best chance of winning the lottery. But somehow at the end of the day they wound up with the #1 pick yet again. A relieved Tomjanovich sighed, "The great thing is that this pick will get a lot of interest back in the Rockets again after an injury-plagued year. In the back of my mind, I kept hoping all of the agony we were going through during the season would pay off somewhere. Right now, we have the opportunity to get that payoff."[17]

As lightning struck twice, the Rockets prayed that the return on their investment would be faster the second time. Therefore they cast their gaze firmly eastward. Like Marco Polo had done a millennium before, the Rockets saw amazing sights that made them dizzy with possibilities. Halfway around the globe, Yao Ming had blossomed into the leading player in all the land. For him, the 2001 season had been the best of times. Performing better than ever, Yao averaged a scintillating 32 points, 19 rebounds, and 4 blocked shots per game.

With eyes wide open, the Rockets made a great leap forward. They picked 22-year-old Yao Ming. This was the first time that a basketball player from an international league was chosen #1 in the NBA draft.

As unlikely as it may seem, lessons can be learned from history. Back in 1971, America's Secretary of State Henry Kissinger engaged in a secret dialogue with China's Premier Chou En-Lai. Soon the world was stunned to discover the political breakthrough they brokered: China's Chairman Mao Tse-tung and US President Richard Nixon announced the normalization of diplomatic relations after twenty years of the Cold War.

Thirty years later, Houston revealed that they too had conducted feverish bargaining sessions. Over the summer, they had covertly paid $350,000 to the Shanghai Sharks for their star player's rights. Following draft day, the Rockets resumed sensitive negotiations with the government of the People's Republic of China (PRC) to seal the deal. But the talks dragged on and Yao's fate was still up in the air. Exhibiting the patience he would soon become known for the world over, Yao told the *Shanghai Morning Post,* "I've already had many frustrations. A few more won't break me."[18]

Finally, nearly three months later on October 20, 2002, basketball history was made. Houston signed Yao to a three-year contract for $12,442,680, with the option to keep him for a fourth year at $5,594,906. Reportedly, Yao would then fork over 30% of his earnings to the Chinese Basketball Association (CBA), 20% to the Chinese government, and a portion of the rest to the Shanghai Sharks. Despite the high-stakes horse-trading, Yao insisted that the money was secondary: "There wasn't anything I really wanted materialistically. For me, if I get paid for one year, I could live on it forever."[19] The real incentive was to meet the challenge of a lifetime, Yao explained:

> Ever since I was very young, I played against players that were much older than me. I was able to hold my own, but I was never able to excel in those competitions. But when I was 17 or 18 years old, I played in basketball camps here in the United States. Knowing I was competing against the best the United States had to offer in the same age group and being able to see I was able to do well against them, I thought, "Wow, I have the potential to be that good." That's when I really started to explore that possibility and to challenge myself that way ... I have never played in an NBA game. I don't know how good I can be. Maybe I'll be a total bust. When you're comparing us and how we measure up to other players in the United States, it's like us using the metric system and you using the English system. You have a

THE TAO OF YAO

sense of what they are. You can understand some of it. But it's only when you are on the same page that you can really measure.[20]

Ultimately Yao concluded, "I want to go to the NBA, because they play a better game. It is where the best players are. My target is to win."[21]

The Rockets' selection was both expected and unexpected. The draft isn't called a lottery for nothing. Many times the #1 pick has been seen as a curse. In hindsight, a team's brain trust often rues the day they selected bright prospects—then helplessly watched them transform from heroes into goats. Choosing Yao elicited a fair share of both skepticism and envy. However, some sage observers had little doubt. Jerry West was one. He owned a spotless track record: a 6'2" Hall of Fame guard for the Los Angeles Lakers, one of the Top 50 players of all time, and the ageless model for the NBA's logo. Testament to his burning desire to win, he remains the only person from the losing team to be named the NBA Finals' MVP. Graduating from coach to general manager, West was the architect of the Lakers' twin championship streaks of 1980s Showtime (led by Kareem and Magic) and the 2000–2002 three-peat (headlined by Shaquille O'Neal and Kobe Bryant). Starting over as the GM of the Memphis Grizzlies, "Mr. Clutch" evaluated the Rockets' choice: "I don't think it is a roll of the dice. He will be a player in the NBA. His size alone is unique; his shooting skill is unique. I think the things he can do as a big player, the coaches will like that. Everyone is looking for a center, so I think that will make him even more valuable."[22]

Certainly it didn't take long for Yao to make his presence felt in the league. Winning the first of undoubtedly many accolades to come, he was named the NBA Western Conference's Rookie of the Month in December 2002. In fifteen games that month, Yao led all rookies by averaging more than 17 points, 10 rebounds, and 2 blocks (grabbing 18 rebounds in a win over San Antonio on December 3, and scoring 29 points with 6 blocks in a win over Indiana on December 18). Yao would repeat as Rookie of the Month in February 2003, ranking first in scoring (16.5 per game) and blocked shots (1.5 per game), and second in rebounding (8.8 per game).

However, before that, he'd go from frying pan into the fire. Not the least of his worries was that he was on a collision course with the perennial All-Star, MVP, and World Champion center Shaquille O'Neal. But more on that later.

As most aspiring rookies are required to do, on May 2, 2002, Yao performed during a perfunctory pre-draft workout to demonstrate his talents before an eager throng of NBA scouts and reporters at Loyola University's Alumni Gym in Chicago. Afterwards he released a prepared but prescient statement. Laying the foundation for his subsequent success, Yao gave a positive impression and set modest expectations. While underplaying his own stature, he respectfully honored the sport, his company, host city, and even the media and the fans. But let's allow the man speak for himself:

THE TAO OF YAO

It's been a dream of mine to play in the NBA ever since the first time I saw a game on TV many years ago. To almost touch that dream today fills me with a sense of joy that words simply cannot describe.

I am humbled and grateful for the unforgettable experience the past few days. I would like first to thank the NBA for hosting this event in the great city of Chicago. The superb organization demonstrates a level of professionalism that I truly admire.

I would also like to express my sincere gratitude to all NBA teams for showing interest in me. I am honored by your presence. And I hope I have not disappointed you with my performance today.

Proper credit is also due to the members of the media. The game of Cat'n'Mouse is stressful, but your resourcefulness and work ethic are something I think we players should emulate. Journalism is a profession I respect a great deal. Just give me some time to warm up. I look forward to taking each and every one of you to dinner sometime in the future. But the check is on you if your reporting makes me look bad.

Last but certainly not least, I owe the greatest debt of gratitude to the fans of basketball everywhere. You gave me the greatest job on earth. And I promise to repay your trust by respecting the game, and by challenging myself to be the best that I can be.

Let the good times roll!

After all Yao's prior commitments to the CBA were fulfilled, Houston could finally say, "Yao has landed" on October 21, 2002. A horde of overjoyed hometown fans rushed to the airport to meet Yao as he touched down. Managing to squeeze out a brief comment during the pandemonium, a flattered Yao beseeched the multitude, "Everyone wants to take pictures but I'm so busy. I just want to say sorry. Sometimes I have to go because I have business to keep."[23]

But his new employers luxuriated in the moment. Witnessing the spectacle, the Rockets' management sensed that the old buzz had returned and realized they had made the right decision. Rockets general counsel Michael Goldberg reminisced about the feeling of déjà vu, "In some ways, it's like standing in The Summit after the seventh game of the first championship. We just won the game. We just won the first championship. Everybody's screaming. There was just a feeling of . . . satisfaction."[24]

Today, reporters constantly roam the field and the locker room in search of news to satisfy an ever more demanding public. Their mission is to ask athletes and coaches their opinions on everything from the weather to politics, but their prayers are answered when they find a reliable source of frank or humorous commentary. The words that fall from a star's lips are treated like manna from heaven and can make such personalities seem even larger than life—whether it be Yogi Berra, Ben Hogan, and John Madden in one era, or Pelé, Wayne Gretzky, and Serena Williams in another.

Yao's debut season in the NBA was an exciting rollercoaster for all involved. He even inspired the most jaded

THE TAO OF YAO

bystanders to track the path of this shooting star, as he shattered stereotypes of all sorts.

In a matter of months, Yao's popularity rivaled that of the prolific actors Jackie Chan and Jet Li. However, Yao's "quotability" and cultural impact elevated him far beyond these entertainers. Game by game, Yao was changing the West's views of him and "foreigners" in general. Meanwhile, he was redefining how Asians could view themselves, as well as the image of the athlete in modern society.

By now, onlookers from around the globe have become familiar with these "Yaoisms." Certainly Yao's statements are memorable in their own right. But they become even more insightful when placed in context with the comments of other esteemed figures: accomplished athletes from past and present, respected coaches (many being former players), and philosophers (from media mavens to ancient sages). Against that rich backdrop of time-honored wisdom from the games of basketball and life, we can better understand not only Yao and but also ourselves.

In addition, coming from a civilization shaped by Taoism, Yao instinctively has introduced its philosophical principles through his words and deeds to fans who find them unusual but fascinatingly provocative. They have the ring of honesty but are wrapped in unfamiliar concepts. As Bill Russell wrote, "Americans are peculiarly blind to the importance of starting points because most of us have grown so accustomed to having ours accepted."[25] But by tracing Yao's statements to their starting point of Taoism, we can view his character and his actions from a fresh perspective that yields remarkable and eternal truths.

"From his cradle to his grave a man never does a single thing which has any FIRST AND FOREMOST object but one—to secure peace of mind, spiritual comfort, for HIMSELF."[2]

—Mark Twain

Chapter 2

The Meaning of the Tao

The Way is the pivot of all things ...[1]
—Lao Tzu

You may ask, "What is the Tao?" or "What does the Tao have to do with Yao?" These are both good questions. The typical Taoist answer would be "everything and nothing." So here's a brief explanation on the relevance of the first half of our title.

The Tao means "the Way" or "the guiding principle" of life. The symbol of the Tao you may recognize more readily than what it actually stands for—a circle divided into two tear-dropped halves, interrelated and ever flowing together. The black is the Yin. The white is the Yang.

They are more than mere opposites. As they say in love, "opposites attract." The Yin and Yang push against each other but pull together to combine into a harmonious whole. The circle represents the continuous cycle of life, and how these two forces always co-exist (note that each side even contains a small circle of the other within itself). The key in life is to have a balance of both Yin and Yang. When a person acquires too much Yin, he is bound to seek equilibrium by then acquiring the necessary Yang, and vice versa.

Tao moves in cycles;
Tao functions through softness.
All is born of something;
Something is born of nothing.[3]

—Lao Tzu

Commonly, the following qualities are ascribed to each half:

Yin	Yang
Dark	Light
Negative	Positive
Evil	Good
Earth	Heaven
Female	Male

Looking at the big picture, Yin and Yang are two sides of the same coin. One cannot be present without the other. In the West, people have historically viewed life as divided into two opposed or even hostile camps, whether they are black vs. white, north vs. south, or left vs. right. However, Taoism views life not in endless opposition but in eternal harmony. That is because Taoism encourages a lifestyle in accord with the rhythms of nature, in sync with the surroundings at large.

> *There are four phenomena of greatness in the universe,*
> *and mankind is one of them.*
> *Mankind follows the ways of the earth,*
> *The earth follows the ways of heaven,*
> *Heaven follows the ways of Tao,*
> *And Tao follows the ways of Nature.*[4]
>
> —Lao Tzu

Initially these cooperative principles were visualized in the elements such as earth and fire and artistically represented in handy organic materials such as wood and stone. Water exemplifies the principles of Taoism. Characterized by smoothly finding the path of least resistance, water is always in motion and adjusts to the environment. Water adapts by changing volume and density, and transforming itself from solid (ice), to liquid (water), to gas (vapor). Water can range from steaming hot to freezing cold, avalanche heavy to snowy light, serenely placid to razor sharp.

In fact, the tempo of a basketball game can be compared to the flow of water. Sometimes the pace is glacially slow, and other times frenetic like a waterfall. No lead is safe, as mercurial swings in momentum can change the outcome of a game in a matter of minutes. A team can be down by 20 points. Then in the time it takes an unwitting fan to make a round trip to and from the concession stand, the team can be up by 20.

In Chinese a person's surname is spoken before their individual name (unlike in English, where one's given name comes before the family name). But just as in other cultures, Chinese parents carefully choose a name for their child that has special positive qualities. Therefore it is interesting that Yao's first name Ming symbolizes the Tao so perfectly. The character "ming" is comprised of two characters: the first means "sun" and the second means "moon".

Sun (pronounced "ri" in Mandarin Chinese) and Moon ("yue") are represented thus:

The written language of Chinese is based upon pictographs that originally depicted objects to convey ideas. One can imagine that the images of the circle and crescent evolved together like so in Chinese:

Standing alone, these words represent the opposites of day and night. But when joined, they enhance each other's characteristics. Combining the light of these opposing heavenly bodies into a complementary pair, "ming" means "bright" both in terms of luminescence and illumination (being smart or enlightened). Together the sun and moon light the world.

Today, people find it unusual to hear any public figure, whether he is an athlete or a politician, voluntarily refuse praise, credit his adversaries, take the blame for mistakes, or admit personal weakness. But here as in other matters, Yao has gone against the grain of conventional behavior.

Quickly proving doubters wrong with his spirited play, Yao received a swelling torrent of praise from respected peers. Nicknamed "The Answer" for his uncanny knack for scoring, the Philadelphia 76ers All-Star point guard Allen Iverson flattered Yao: "He's special. He's a gift from God."[5]

But Yao was not shy about owning up to his shortcomings. When asked to explain how a disappointing defeat happened, Yao shrugged, "I don't know why. Help me find an excuse."[6] He went on to say, "I guess bad shooting is contagious. Tonight, it was like SARS."[7] The next day, after suffering a dismal fourth quarter that led to another loss, Yao sheepishly remembered feeling, "I just wanted to get home pretty quick, as quickly as possible."[8]

Those on tiptoe don't stand up,
those who take long strides don't walk;
those who see themselves are not perceptive,
those who assert themselves are not illustrious;
those who glorify themselves have no merit,
those who are proud of themselves do not last.[9]
                                        —Lao Tzu

Keeping the game in perspective, Yao described a win after a long losing streak: "It's like the sun coming out after a long rain. It was a very heavy atmosphere."[10] Since Yao managed to keep both his anger and his excitement in check, he was admired for his equanimity.

Graduating from Loyola Marymount University, Rick Adelman was picked #79 by the San Diego Rockets in 1968. Chosen by Portland in the 1970 NBA Expansion Draft, the 6'2" guard concluded his career with the Kansas City-Omaha Kings in 1975. Now as the Sacramento Kings' coach, Adelman remarked of Yao: "I just watch his composure. And he's really very even-keeled. He has up games, but he's not down after he has a tough game. He keeps playing. He's very gracious to the people he plays against, but he's a competitor. You could have a situation that could be very tough, but he could handle it."[11]

Yao described his perspective: "There will always be people who will criticize me and that's something I can't think about.... When I'm being criticized, I try not to listen to it, but when I play well, I'll remember that I might not play very well in the next game."[12] Being grounded is essential, since Yao noted, "In one game, I can make it up all the way up to heaven and then I can go all the way back down to hell."[13]

Tomjanovich appreciated Yao's approach. "He doesn't like to embarrass people. He does things the right way."[14] So did Jeff Van Gundy. Having inherited the coaching bug from his father, he diligently climbed up through the coaching ranks. Assisting Rick Pitino at Providence, Van Gundy soon was advising marquee NBA generals such as Pat Riley, John McLeod, and Don Nelson in New York. Finally getting the chance that most coaches wait their whole lifetimes for, he inherited the helm of the Knicks in 1996 at the tender age of 34.

Van Gundy survived the pressure cooker of the back-biting Big Apple only to suddenly resign in 2001 when he said, "I'm going to step back and exhale for the first time in 13 years."[15] When he became an analyst for the cable channel TNT the following year, Van Gundy praised Tomjanovich's prized recruit: "The thing I love about Yao is his demeanor. He has the intensity and competitive spirit of a great player. I know he has the size and the skills, and defensively, he's not nearly as proficient as he needs to be. But that demeanor is going to help him through his great moments and his not-so-great moments."[16]

Yao concurred, "When you have pitiful moments, that makes the good moments more valuable."[17] In a practical sense, Yao, like water itself, embodies the Tao. Confronting hurdles at every turn, he stays the course and keeps moving forward: "It is hard to pick out the one part that has been the hardest. I've had ups and downs like the waves of the ocean."[18] The wise Lao Tzu would have sympathized with him.

The best [man] is like water.
Water is good; it benefits all things and does not compete with
    them.
It dwells in [lowly] places that all disdain.
This is why it is so near to Tao.[19]

—Lao Tzu

THE TAO OF YAO

Chapter 3

The Wisdom of Lao

When the highest type of men hear Tao,
They diligently practice it.
When the average type of men hear Tao,
They half believe in it.
When the lowest type of men hear Tao,
They laugh heartily at it.[1]

—Lao Tzu

Now, you may wonder, who is this Lao who is responsible for these sayings about Taoism? And what does he have to do with Yao?

Well, the specifics of Lao Tzu's life are very hazy and hotly debated. Historians still disagree whether "The Old Master" was even an actual person. But as the story goes, Lao was a venerated scholar who lived during the later part of the Chou Dynasty (1123–256 B.C.) and was a contemporary of Confucius (551–479 B.C.). Lao lived in a time of unrest, a period known as the "Warring States" (475–221 B.C.). China's longest dynasty had once commanded two hundred loyal states. But after combating both barbarians and rebellions, the Chou had less than fifteen at its end.[2]

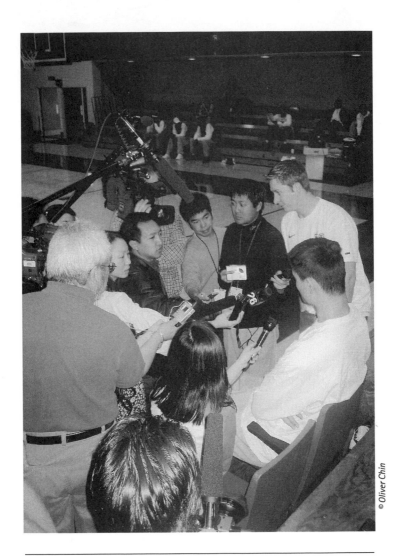

© Oliver Chin

◄ Yao's teammates watch him hold court.

"[Yao's] not like an American player. All these cameras following him around, he could care less about them."[3]

—Steve Francis

THE TAO OF YAO

However, Lao's teachings survived this tumultuous period and were incorporated into the venerated book *Tao Te Ching*, destined to influence generations of Chinese thought ever since.

This collection of essays, titled in translation *Classic of the Way and Virtue* or *The Book of the Way*, is second only to the Bible in how many times it has been translated throughout history (the citations in this book draw upon at least four different versions). The *Tao Te Ching*'s eighty-one concise chapters advise readers how to think and act in a spectrum of situations. In both abstract and concrete terms, Lao shows one the proper way to live in harmony with the "Will of Heaven," and how to govern in accordance with the "Will of the People."

To this day people are inspired by Lao's words and appreciate the relevance to their personal lives and current events. However, just as often, his aphorisms are casually treated like fortune cookie clichés. Similarly, the press has treated Yao's comments both with startled appreciation and sarcastic cynicism. It is no coincidence that Yao's words are modern descendants of Lao's own. A comparison of the words of both men yields insights as relevant to the present as to the past.

Unique in his approach, Lao suggests that any person can achieve harmony with nature through the act of "nondoing." The ideal of emptiness or "doing nothing" is baffling to many Westerners. For example, Western culture praises those who act first and ask questions later, or are "go-getters" and "pro-active." Doing something, even if it is impulsive, ill-conceived, or simply wrong in the end, is often seen as better than doing nothing at all. Truly in the present day and age, impatience is a virtue. But Lao would say that sometimes one learns more by doing nothing (i.e., by observing) than by jumping mindlessly into the middle of the fray.

That is why Yao's comments seem so peculiar to Westerners: they epitomize this wholly different frame of mind. For example, every professional athlete wants to be a starting player. Who would want to be a backup, when being a benchwarmer puts you one step closer to watching from the bleachers? Here Yao defies the usual pattern and looks at the bright side of what others would consider a bad situation. After a night where he only played fifteen minutes, Yao pondered, "I haven't had the opportunity to play a lot in the game. I hope to play more. It's definitely different to sit on the bench and watch the game. It's a different feeling. I can see the situation on the court when I'm sitting on the bench."[4]

In his version of the Tao, Stephen Mitchell writes that Lao's

... insistence on *wei wu wei*, literally "doing non-doing,"... has been seen as passivity. Nothing could be further from the truth.

A good athlete can enter a state of body-awareness in which the right stroke or the right movement happens by itself, effortlessly, without any interference of the conscious will. This is a paradigm for non-action: the purest and most effective form of action. The game plays the game; the poem writes the poem; we can't tell the dancer from the dance.

Less and less do you need to force things,
until finally you arrive at non-action.
When nothing is done,
nothing is left undone.
[Lao Tzu, *Tao Te Ching*, Chapter 48]

Nothing is done because the doer has wholeheartedly vanished into the deed; the fuel has been completely transformed into the flame. This "nothing" is, in fact, everything. It happens when we trust the intelligence of the universe in the same way that an athlete or a dancer trusts the superior intelligence of the body.[5]

The ferocious competitor Bill Russell agreed: "At that special level all sorts of odd things happened. The game would be in the white heat of competition, and yet somehow I wouldn't feel competitive—which is a miracle in itself. I'd be putting out the maximum effort, straining, coughing up parts of my lungs as we ran, and yet I never felt the pain."[6]

Those who know others are wise;
those who know themselves are enlightened.[7]
—Lao Tzu

From the moment Yao stepped off the airplane and onto the Houston tarmac, he knew what he was getting into: "I know I made everybody wait a long time. I hope everybody will think it was worth the wait ... I hope that my hard work, I can meet everybody's expectations ... I can't wait. I can't wait to get into camp and play."[8]

But quickly Yao realized that life gets hotter under the constant glare of the camera lights. "It seems like I've been magnified much larger than I actually am. Everybody's looking at me."[9] At a post-game press conference, Yao asserted, "I think the greatest pressure comes from other people's hopes and expectations of me. I think I gave myself more time to achieve certain things than other people do."[10]

Through the statements, conduct, and example of a modern basketball phenomenon, words written millennia ago find renewed relevance. Yao's statements have seemed profound precisely because they dovetail so well with those of one of the most respected philosophers in human history.

The Way is unimpeded harmony;
its potential may never be fully exploited.
It is as deep as the source of all things....[11]
—Lao Tzu

Yao Ming frequently provokes a number of perplexed looks with statements like this: "I remember very clearly something my math teacher said to me when I was young: The hardest challenges sometimes are the ones you will get right, and the easiest ones are sometimes the ones you will mess up."[12] Many found this observation ridiculous since they consider the concepts polar opposites. But according to Lao Tzu, "Words of truth seem contradictory."[13] In the context of the Taoist cycle of Yin and Yang, Lao enlightens us that "difficult and easy are complementary."[14]

Begin the most difficult task in the world while it is still easy.
Begin the greatest task in the world while it is still small.
That is how the Sage becomes great without striving.
One who makes promises easily is inevitably unreliable.
One who thinks everything is easy inevitably finds everything
    difficult.
That is why the Sage alone regards everything as difficult
and in the end finds no difficulty at all. [15]

— Lao Tzu

From this viewpoint it does make sense that if one tackles
a challenge before it becomes too large, one can achieve
greater things with relative ease. By understanding the basic
Taoist relationship between difficult and easy, Yao was able
to draw upon Lao's timeless wisdom for comfort in the here
and now.

Things flourish, and each returns to its root.
Returning to the root is called tranquility;
This is what is meant by returning to one's basic nature.
Returning to one's basic nature is called constancy.
To understand constancy is called enlightening. [16]

— Lao Tzu

Undoubtedly Yao needed a constant nature to endure a year
that would be not only more trying but more gratifying than
he could have ever imagined.

"By hero, we tend to mean a heightened man who, more than other men, possesses qualities of courage, loyalty, resourcefulness, charisma, above all, selflessness. He is an example of right behavior; the sort of man who risks his life to protect his society's values, sacrificing his personal needs for those of the community.... There is, of course, another sort of heightened man who bulks large in the popular imagination.... He is not "loyal," not a model of right behavior. Quite the contrary, he fascinates because he undermines the expected order. He possesses the qualities of the "hero": skill, resourcefulness, courage, intelligence. But he is the opposite of selfless. He is hungry; "heightened," not as an example, but as a presence, a phenomenon of sheer energy. One thinks of certain sports heroes, who boast and indulge their whims; who cannot be relied on, not because they are treacherous, but because the order of their needs is purely idiosyncratic."[1]

—Paul Zweig

THE TAO OF YAO

Chapter 4

The Cultural Ambassador

Be content with what you have; rejoice in the way things are.
When you realize there is nothing lacking, the whole world
belongs to you.[2]

—Lao Tzu

There is a lot of pressure on me. This is the most pressure I've ever
faced in my life, but it's something I have to deal with.[3]

—Yao Ming

Throughout his life, Yao was accustomed to being the center of attention. Becoming the leading basketball player from the world's most populous nation of 1.3 billion people was no small feat. So when asked about the difference between playing basketball in China versus in America, Yao blithely replied, "They speak Chinese in China. They speak English here."[4]

However, Yao intuitively recognized that he was about to enter a new dimension of both scrutiny and fame. Repeatedly asked how he was affected by the expectations placed on him by his countrymen, Yao stated, "It is a bit of a burden on me, but I have to realize it's a responsibility I have to shoulder."[5]

Joining her son in Houston at the start of his rookie season, Fang Feng Di encapsulated Yao's predicament. "There are so many people watching him, I am proud of him, but I also worry. People can see it how they want to see it. Whatever somebody sees is their truth."[6] She knew best, as she provided the following reminder, "A mother knows her son."[7]

Soon Yao arrived at the same conclusion: "I don't know what people think. Whatever they think is what I am."[8]

If you want to accord with the Tao,
just do your job, then let go.[9]

—Lao Tzu

Truly, Yao became a prism through which a variety of parties projected their own interests and agendas. Fielding a burgeoning list of demands on his time, Yao reiterated his desire to concentrate on his day job: "I am a basketball player, and I would like to focus my energy on basketball. The other things, I would rather not do. It is not something that I am greatly interested in, but I know it is my responsibility."[10] Yet with a diplomatic flair, Yao manages to address and balance the competing social, political, and economic causes of three major constituencies: the country of China, the NBA, and Asians all across America.

National Pride

Just realize where you come from:
this is the essence of wisdom.[11]

—Lao Tzu

Eager to embark on his new NBA adventure, Yao remarked, "I'm used to Chinese things, and I love Chinese things, but I also love new experiences."[12] The ideal spokesman for his homeland, Yao personifies China's potential for both rapid progress and international influence. Having long considered itself the "Middle Kingdom," the center of civilization, China has lately been playing catch-up. Most notably, in 1966 Chairman Mao Tse-tung blamed the West for infecting China's culture. In this "Cultural Revolution," he mobilized the populace to eradicate all trace of Western influences, to punish the Westernized among them, and to "re-educate" the rest. It took China nearly two decades to recover from such self-destructive policies. Now craving competitive respect in the twenty-first century, China's leadership has actively engaged the economic powers of the West, but tries to maintain absolute political control at home.

However, trade is a two-way street, and China and the United States have had their fair share of collisions in the past century. The clashes include the Boxer Rebellion, the Korean War, the Cold War, the Cultural Revolution, and the ongoing dispute over the recognition of Taiwan. Recently there was the 1999 US bombing of the Chinese embassy in Belgrade, the 1999 US indictment of scientist Wen Ho Lee in the hunt for Chinese spies at Los Alamos nuclear laboratories, the 2001 Chinese capture of a US spy plane that shot down a PRC fighter jet, and another US 2003 indictment of a Chinese informant whom the FBI had paid $1.7 million but who was accused of being a double agent for the Chinese government.

Nevertheless, China has lobbied to become fully accepted

← "The great social adventure of America is no longer the conquest of the wilderness but the absorption of fifty different peoples."[13]

—Walter Lippmann, 1914

into the world community, and to overcome its poor international reputation for both human rights and diplomacy. Intolerant of dissent, the regime viciously extinguished pro-democracy demonstrators in Tiananmen Square in 1989 (the US responded with temporary economic sanctions). Mindful that Karl Marx, the founder of communism, derided religion as "the opiate of the masses," China has mercilessly persecuted Tibetan Buddhists as well as the cult Falun Gong. Despite this conduct, in 2000 the US supported China's accession into the World Trade Organization, an international consortium that promotes economic globalization. Because of its vital role in commerce (the world's fifth largest economy is predicted to climb to second only to the US by 2030), China was eventually accepted in August 2002.[14] With two-way trade that exceeds $90 billion annually, the US is China's second-largest trading partner after Japan, and China is the US' fourth-largest partner following Canada, Mexico, and Japan.[15]

In 1997, China lobbied to become the host nation for the 2008 Summer Olympics. Despite protests by Amnesty International claiming that "More people were executed in China in the last three months than in the rest of the world for the last three years," in July 2001 China won its bid. To take full advantage of this promotional opportunity, China immediately started clean-up and construction projects to showcase its progress to the world. However, the best-laid plans can go awry. In 2003 the PRC systematically chose to deny that it had severe AIDS (Acquired Immune Deficiency Syndrome) and SARS (Severe Acute Respiratory Syndrome) epidemics. Only when the true extent of these problems was exposed were these stances hastily discredited. Such ill-advised "damage control" has backfired terribly, with a tremendous cascade of economic, social, and political fallout.

So it is rather amazing to see how one man could become such a celebrated medium of positive dialogue between two cultures prone to conflict. Perhaps this feat was made easier in an era of high technology. Even in societies that restrict citizen access to information and censor speech, people indulge in their addiction to Western pop culture via satellite television, telecommunications, and bootlegged multimedia. "I've had seven cellphones already myself. China is changing and developing at a rapid pace," said Yao. "All I can say is that I hope my development as a basketball player can match that. While China learns more about the world, I hope that the world will also learn more about China."[16]

Ironically, Yao represents stereotypical Eastern values to Western observers, when China itself is undergoing Westernization at a breakneck pace. To fix China's moribund economy, in 1978 Premier Deng Xiao Ping began to encourage a cottage capitalism. Justifying his radical policy—which Mao would have deemed heretical—Deng claimed that it fit under the umbrella of communism. By July 1, 1997, China would complete the long-anticipated annexation of the former British colony of Hong Kong. Absorbing this capital of capitalism with a policy called "one country, two systems" was the culmination of Deng's strategy to westernize China's agriculture-based economy. By the sixth anniversary of the handover, China had provided Hong Kong an advantageous free-trade agreement with the mainland, but was pressuring

Hong Kong to pass stricter laws to stifle dissent. This provoked wide-scale public demonstrations in July 2003 that local officials acknowledged were the largest here since the protests against the PRC's brutal crackdown in Tiananmen Square on June 4, 1989.[17]

The Chinese have taken other steps to transform their nation. In 1979, China tackled its immense problem of overpopulation. Flying in the face of Chinese tradition, the PRC abolished large families by imposing its "one child per family" rule and harshly forced compliance by sterilizing parents who bore two children. More than twenty years later, China took another audacious step: to convert its rural population into an urban one. Lagging behind the average of industrialized nations and the world at large, China saw its relatively low urban population as another embarrassing symbol of backwardness. Reversing it was a commitment to progress. Therefore, China decreed that its percentage of citizens who lived in cities would rise from 30% to 60% by 2025. Yao's hometown of Shanghai epitomized this conversion, as ancient neighborhoods were razed and replaced by gleaming skyscrapers. The scale of this change and its effects will be enormous: the projected influx of more than 300 million peasants from the countryside is greater than the entire US population.

China's desire for increased economic growth has required it to break the "iron rice bowl," its social contract that promised lifetime employment for every worker and food for every mouth. Seeking Western progress, the PRC has encountered intractable problems. The shift from state-owned heavy industry to privatized ownership has led to an unpredictable entrepreneurial free-for-all and resulted in overcrowded urban centers that already are coping with wide-scale unemployment and strained social services. This problematic push for economic growth is symbolized by the $25 billion Three Gorges Dam on the Yangtze River. Built in hopes of providing 10% of China's energy needs, this mega-development project stretches five times the width of the Hoover Dam. It will create an upriver reservoir that stretches a distance equal to that from Los Angeles to San Francisco. The dam will force 1.3 million people to relocate and cause unprecedented environmental degradation.

In this uncertain climate, China has lionized a goodwill ambassador who exudes optimism in the future and patriotism for his country. Yao's exploits are recounted religiously in China, especially in his hometown, where Yao's Shanghai Sharks coach, Li Zhangmin, called his former player "The Pride of Shanghai." Reporting for the daily paper *The Xin Min Evening News*, sportswriter Yan Xiao Xian declared, "It's like a dream come true. A lot of young people are crazy about him. He's like a national hero."[18]

In a nation where few citizens are allowed to go abroad (for fear of mass exodus as well as a brain drain), athletes are some of China's highest-profile citizens. When government sports officials first spotted this growing boy they knew they could take no chances. Another Shanghai coach, Wang Qun, remembered Yao:

> He was only 12 but already 6-5. We knew he would keep growing. We didn't trust the lower-level sports schools. We wanted him here so our specialists could make sure

he got enough to eat and sleep and that his bones were growing properly. Everybody else ate in the cafeteria, but Yao ate in a special kitchen reserved for champions. Only Olympics and world competition winners could eat there.[19]

Donn Nelson, the Dallas Mavericks assistant coach and director of player personnel (and whose father Don is the head coach), corroborated that Yao was a prized graduate of China's highly selective system of sports training. "A lot of those guys have the chance to work with the best resources and the best people at a very early age. They're considered invaluable assets to their countries."[20] To make it to the top, Chinese athletes are not only drilled in their specialties from an early age but coached to say the right things. Like actors, their success is dependent on following the script provided, and performing to make their government look as good as possible.

Definitely Yao has been a model representative, since the PRC's retribution is as swift for an athlete's defiance as for a protestor's. Wang Zhi Zhi won great acclaim as the first Chinese basketball player to enter the NBA. But when Wang (now a member of the Los Angeles Clippers) refused to play for China in the 2002 summer Asian Games, the government quickly banned the broadcasting of all Clippers games in China for the 2002–03 season. Meanwhile, Yao has been careful to meet his obligations to the Chinese government and to keep his conduct above board. "I know that many Chinese fans are watching my games and are interested in my progress," understated Yao.[21]

Knowing that a lot rides on his performance, Yao put things into perspective: "I'm not the only thing that is exciting about China. There are a lot of things about China that are exciting. I'm just doing what I always do and doing what I think I should do. I don't think it's a burden. But if people can learn something from that, that's great."[22] In the end Yao came to terms dealing with such responsibility. "I feel a lot of pressure on me. But I feel it every day. I am used to it."[23]

He got some words of encouragement from a living legend who'd been there and done that. After three comebacks from retirement, Michael Jordan finally decided to call it quits just as Yao began his voyage. Over his fifteen-year career, 6'6" Jordan started as Rookie of the Year in 1985 and left as arguably the greatest player in NBA history. Along the way, Jordan was a perpetual MVP: he won the award for each of the Chicago Bulls' six championships, five regular seasons, and three of his eleven All-Star games. Owning the highest career scoring average (31.5 points per game) and membership in eight all-defensive teams, he earned two Olympic gold medals in 1984 and 1992. Immortalized on countless Nike sneakers and advertisements, Jordan became the NBA's golden goose by generating billions in revenue for countless corporations. Making more money through endorsements than through his salary, he amassed a net worth of $400 million by the time he hung up his Air Jordans. Beyond all these accolades, MJ was, hands down, the most popular athlete in China.

After playing Yao for the first time in his farewell season, Jordan empathized with him: "It's tough for him to have all that responsibility, not just in basketball, but socially.

> "Millions of Chinese, young and old, basketball buffs and novices, are dodging work, skipping class and losing sleep to catch a glimpse of the towering, young Shanghai native who dunked his way out of this country's fledgling basketball league and onto the shimmering stage of the NBA as [the 2002] No. 1 draft pick."[24]
>
> —*Washington Post*

He's got the government and all of China. Let the basketball be his haven to relax and go out and enjoy himself. Once you're on the basketball court, that's your peace. That's where no one can really bother you. That's when you can express yourself."[25]

Well, that's partially true. As long as you play for the NBA, every game is serious business. Magic Johnson fondly remembered his coach Pat Riley saying, "Basketball is a business. If you want to have fun, go to the YMCA."[26]

The Houston Globetrotters

Grasp the great image and the world will come to you;
coming to you they are not harmed,
for peace and harmony will be great.[27]

—Lao Tzu

Following his first meeting with Yao at NBA headquarters in New York, NBA commissioner David Stern waxed, "Mostly, I just wanted to tell Yao we're proud of him. He is answering a thousand questions, the same ones heard so many times, with dignity, grace and good humor, and we recognize the burden he is under. He is very much an ambassador both ways. America is learning things about the People's Republic of China, and a lot of people in China are learning about America through him."[28]

The NBA's Asia spokeswoman Sau Ching Cheong echoed Stern's sentiments: "I think to people in China, or for that matter Chinese the world over, Yao Ming has transcended sports. He is definitely an inspiration to all people in China. He has given them a sense that they can go out in the world and succeed."[29] But make no mistake about it, the NBA has benefited greatly from Yao's success.

Back in 1950, the four major American professional sports leagues couldn't care less about what inspired other countries. Like hot dogs and apple pie, each league was born and bred for American tastes, with less than 5% of its players born overseas. Fifty years later, they have come around to see the world as their oyster, and are as likely to put nachos and sushi on the menu as french fries and hamburgers. In 2002, the percentage of foreign players was 31.6% for the National Hockey League, 25% for Major League Baseball, 14.5% for the NBA, and 2.4% for the National Football League (proof of how the rest of the world considers soccer "football"). But for the first three leagues, their percentages doubled within the past decade alone.[30]

In the NBA, what was once a trickle now has become a flood. From Africa came the centers Olajuwon from Nigeria, Manute Bol (the 7'7" walking stick from the war-torn Sudan), and Dikembe Mutombo from Zaire. Following the fall of

THE TAO OF YAO

the Berlin Wall in the 1990s, the first wave of players arrived from Eastern Europe: the late Croatian guard Drazen Petrovic, Serbian center Vlade Divac, Lithuanian guard Sarunas Marciulionis, Croatian forward Toni Kukoc, and Lithuanian center Arvydas Sabonis.

Inspired by their success, teams deployed a network of scouts to scour the globe for the next big thing. Starting the 2002–03 season, the NBA's percentage of non-American players climbed to over 17%, triple the total five years before. This included sixty-five foreign players from thirty-four countries, enough personnel to fully staff five of the twenty-nine team rosters.[31] In the 2002 draft, Yao was by no means alone: there were twelve international players among the fifty-two players chosen, including five of the first sixteen picks. The game that Dr. James Naismith invented in Springfield, Massachusetts, in the winter of 1891 with two peach baskets and a soccer ball now resembled the United Nations.

Also an assistant with the Lithuanian national team, Donn Nelson helped his father Don bring over Marciulionis to play for the Golden State Warriors in 1989, and import Wang Zhi Zhi from the CBA's Bayi Rockets to Dallas in 2000. "I think what we're seeing is a natural phenomenon. Look at the popularity of the game around the world since the '92 Olympics and the fact that the best athletes in other countries are gravitating toward basketball," said Nelson. "Then, the underage American players coming into the league are not ready, and that poses a big problem for coaches and general managers. The situation lends itself to the foreign markets."[32]

At the NBA's 2002 preseason program that welcomed incoming rookies, ex-Houston Rocket Kenny Smith declared that the drafting of foreign players was merely a temporary trend. "If you look over the years, if a team wins the championship with a big guard, everyone wants a big guard," he said. "When Detroit won with three guards, everyone wanted three guards. Now Dirk Nowitzki had a great year and [people are saying], 'Let's see if we can find another Dirk.' It's a vogue thing to draft a European player. . . . Are these players better? I don't think so. They are different, but does different mean better?"[33]

Speedy Portland Trail Blazers guard Damon Stoudamire thinks otherwise. Rookie of the Year in 1994–95, Stoudamire observed the evolving attitude of foreign players up close. "They aren't afraid anymore. They can play and they know it. I used to think this was a fad. I don't anymore. I think American players should be worried."[34] On the topic of whether American players or fans would be xenophobic, Yao optimistically replied, "There are so many successful foreign players in the NBA. I don't think they'll mind another one."[35]

Fittingly, Yao admired one of his NBA predecessors, Arvydas Sabonis, saying, "Gold will always shine. That's how I'd like to describe Sabonis."[36] Yao modeled his play after his childhood idol: "I like the way he uses his mind, the way he passes. He can play inside and outside. He's got a three-point shot, and I remember him dunking over David

---

The vanguard of a new generation of global basketball stars, Dirk ▶ Nowitzki and Kobe Bryant square off.

THE TAO OF YAO

Robinson. He's very smart. I like the way his mind allows him to get the best of each situation."[37] Still a productive center with Portland, the 7'3" 300-lb "Sabas" complimented Yao but advised him to take notes, saying, "He is a good player. But good players need time to learn. He needs to be here to learn against the best players in the world."[38] This was sound advice. When Yao finally got to play against his hero on November 26, 2002, he got schooled. The wily Sabonis threw his weight around and rudely blocked Yao's shot en route to a 77–71 win over the Rockets. This forced the youngster to reconsider his own stature. "I think I need to eat more," Yao mulled.[39]

Meanwhile league officials saw a great bounty in Yao. Terry Lyons, NBA vice president of international public relations, said, "Every person he interacts with comes away impressed by what a great guy he is. You don't see that very often. He has a dignity, style, and charisma that you can't teach."[40] Elsewhere Lyons commented, "Wang Zhi Zhi kind of set the table, but if that's the case, then Yao Ming is sitting down for a big meal. His impact on basketball in China and in Asia will be like no player ever."[41]

"Kids are going to want to be like Yao—now," proclaimed NBA Commissioner Stern.[42] For a man who has the resources of a global marketing machine at his disposal, those words were a self-fulfilling prophecy. Like many other multinational corporations after many years of growth, the NBA had faced a saturated US market and a future of sluggish TV ratings, attendance, and enthusiasm over a product that now appeared rife with players long on ego but short on class. Looking overseas for expansion was not just

> "Just as he has changed the opinion of many who doubted him early, Yao has also altered the NBA's marketing approach in a fundamental way.... He has become hugely popular here for his pleasant nature, unselfishness, work habits and humility."[43]
> —*The New York Times*

an option, it was a necessity. Previously Magic, Bird and Jordan had become international stars in countries they've never heard of, much less visited. But now the league not only needed talented foreign players but also their paying fan base that came with them. Since 1987, the NBA has expanded into TV sets in 212 countries and 42 different languages around the world ... but it still wanted more. "We're running out of countries," said Andrew Messick, the NBA's senior international vice president.[44]

For his part, Stern sized up his large guest as the NBA's next meal ticket: "Put him back into a broader perspective. He's another step in the internationalization of the game. We went from Dirk Nowitzki, to Paul Gasol, to Emanuel Ginobili, for us to see representatives of star level from Eastern and Western Europe, South America, and now Asia."[45] Upon finally meeting his boss at the NBA headquarters in New York, Yao lampooned his diminutive stature: "Usually when I've seen him, I've seen him behind a podium. I didn't know he was that short."[46] But he did recognize Stern's oversized ambition and knew better than to ask the following question: "I wanted to ask if he planned to expand NBA basketball to the moon."[47]

Yao is China's best basketball export to date. But more importantly he is also the NBA's best import back into China. He is the ultimate Trojan Horse for the world's biggest consumer market. Through Yao the NBA could bring other companies into China to market their brands and build their businesses. Rich Thomaselli, a writer for *Advertising Age*, frankly assessed Stern's bonanza in an article for *Sports Illustrated*: "Yao comes along at the perfect time to the perfect league. The NBA has wanted exponential global growth. The other foreign players have helped, but Yao, who is truly unique because of his size, background, and personality, will lead the way."[48]

Yao's payoff for the NBA in China has been immediate. In one year NBA TV contracts climbed from five to fourteen, including one with the dominant state-run station China Central Television (CCTV) to feature the NBA game of the week.[49] Even by the All-Star break, Yao's peers recognized that their employer had effectively crowned him Jordan's successor as a global sports icon. Shaq said, "It's a changing of the guard," and Indiana Pacers forward Jermaine O'Neal added, "He's a moneymaker for all the players in the NBA."[50]

The league and its teams were ready to ride this new Rocket to a windfall of profits. Hoping to draw new fans from the San Francisco Bay Area (where in many counties Asians constitute at least one-quarter of the population), the Golden State Warriors immediately unveiled its "Got Yao?" promotion. To boost attendance, it marketed a "mini-plan" using Yao's arrivals as cornerstones to package ticket sales for multiple games, printing advertisements in both English and Chinese. The Warriors' chief operating officer Robert

Rowell said, "Our goal this year is to grow ticket sales 8 to 10 percent, and of that growth we want 2 percent to come from the Asian community."[51] The strategy worked, as Yao's two games had 25% more fans than their season average, and his last game had the biggest crowd of the year (surpassing even Michael Jordan's farewell visit).[52]

Of course, Houston was in the driver's seat. On Yao's first evening at the Rockets' stadium, the Compaq Center (in an era of corporate sponsorship, the new name for The Summit), Coach Rudy Tomjanovich was sanguine on the task before him: "I've had the opportunity to coach some of the greatest players ever, but to also be entrusted with the development of the first great Asian player is a privilege."[53] But Les Alexander's eyes flashed dollar signs. No stranger to self-promotion, the Rockets' owner gushed, "This is going to be the biggest individual sports story of all time." For those unclear on what he meant, Alexander predicted, "[Yao will be] bigger than Michael Jordan in the world; not in the US but in the world. There are so many Asians, he'll be the biggest athlete of all time."[54]

Accordingly the Rockets' new slogan for their 2002 season was "Be Part of Something Big," which they trumpeted in a publicity campaign that plastered Yao on billboards, television, and newspapers. Hiring four Chinese employees who spoke Mandarin, the Rockets produced "The Big Hour," the first NBA radio show in Mandarin, which ran weekly on Saturdays at 3 PM. For the show Yao taped a 10-minute interview, which was also translated into English on the Rockets' website. Catering to the international Chinese audience, Rockets' President George Postolos explained, "What they are starved for is Yao Ming content, and we're producing it. We're going to find a way to get it to them for promotional purposes, because we know we benefit from people saying this is the most watched team in the world, this is the most popular team in the world, this is China's team."[55]

At the gate Yao's impact was also instantaneous. In the 2002 season, the Rockets' television ratings rose over 60% from the year before.[56] Regarding his effect on league ticket sales, Yao deferred comment by saying simply, "I don't really understand that very well. I am a basketball player, not a businessman."[57] However, the Rockets' Publicity Director Nelson Luis did understand. He estimated that the Rockets website's traffic rose 300% since Yao donned his #11 uniform. But more importantly, Houston averaged almost 20% more attendees per game than the previous season average of 11,700. Selling 2,000 more tickets at an average price greater than $25, Yao was responsible for nearly $2 million in Houston's increased attendance revenue in his first year alone. Since the NBA's average attendance was higher than Houston's sellout capacity of 16,285 at the Compaq Center, the Rockets were glad that they had already planned to move at the start of the 2003 season into the new Houston Arena, which holds 18,500 customers.

Meanwhile back in Asia, Chinese brewers Yanjing Beer signed a $1 million marketing campaign with the Rockets that revolves around Yao.[58] Aware that both a nation and a league had invested their hopes in him, Yao stated, "Either burden is too heavy for me to stand it. So it doesn't matter which one is heavier. I will try my best to make myself a student of basketball."[59] Soon he would realize that he bore the dear dreams of a multitude of Asian and Chinese Americans as well.

Coming to America

A great nation receives all that flows into it.[60]
—Lao Tzu

To commemorate Yao's first visit, the Miami Heat gave away free fortune cookies to fans attending the game. When asked about this curious promotion, Yao surmised, "First of all, there's no such thing as a fortune cookie in China. Second, I think maybe fortune cookies are too small. They should give out something bigger."[61] He was right. Chinese Americans invented fortune cookies in San Francisco in the early 1900s. Introduced into China only a decade ago, the snack is primarily served to foreign tourists. This marketing mix-up was emblematic of the experience of Chinese Americans: they straddle two cultures but are questioned as to where they really belong.

The American Dream continues to be a powerful idea, drawing people the world over to the nation's shores. People come to the United States because they aspire to be free, as the Declaration of Independence claims, to "enjoy life, liberty, and the pursuit of happiness." Then, depending on their own hard work, skill, and luck, they hope to build a flourishing life for themselves and their families.

With this ideal in mind, in America sports has become much more than a unifying pastime for a diverse society; it is a gateway for minorities to be accepted by the majority. If

YAO MING BIG 3 MINI-PLAN

**Featuring Yao Ming,
the NBA's #1 draft pick in 2002**

Wed	Nov 27	Houston	7:30 p.m.
Tues	Dec 3	Denver	7:30 p.m.
Sat	Dec 7	Dallas	7:30 p.m.

**3 GREAT games. Same GREAT seats.
GREAT package price!**

GENERAL SEATING:

Per Seat	Package Price
$60.00	$180.00
$48.00	$144.00
$34.00	$102.00
$30.00	$90.00
$22.00	$66.00

YAO MING BIG 7 MINI-PLAN

Wed	Nov 27	Houston	7:30 p.m.
Tues	Dec 10	L.A. Lakers	7:30 p.m.
Mon	Jan 20	Sacramento	1:00 p.m.
Thurs	Jan 23	New Jersey	7:00 p.m.
Tues	Feb 18	Boston	7:30 p.m.
Fri	Mar 14	Dallas	7:30 p.m.

PLUS
**Houson Rockets
Friday, March 21 at 7:30 p.m.**
FOR FREE!

**See Yao Ming twice at The Arena in Oakland
this season in our exclusive club seating,
PLUS the World Champion L.A. Lakers!**

CLUB SEATING:

Per Seat	Package Price
$105.00	$630.00
$78.00	$468.00
$68.00	$408.00

CLICK AND ROLL ON **WARRIORS.COM**
OR CALL **1-888-GSW-HOOP** (OPTION 1)
IT'S A GREAT TIME OUT!
TO SECURE YOUR SEATS TODAY!

© Golden State Warriors

"It was a great deal of fun to play in the San Francisco area.... I could feel the warmth coming from the people, and it means a lot to have their support. But I can tell if I were playing there instead of Houston, there would be much more pressure on me."[62]

—Yao Ming

THE TAO OF YAO

given an equal opportunity to succeed on a level playing field, an athlete inspires his or her community to believe that others can achieve similar respect and reward in daily life. Therefore, athletes motivate citizens both to maintain faith in "making it" and to see sports as a viable path to rise in economic class and social stature.

Think Jim Thorpe in football. Jesse Owens in the Olympics. Jack Johnson and Joe Louis in boxing.

Today the exploits of Annika Sorenstam revive the legacy of Mildred "Babe" Didrikson Zacharias in women's golf. When tennis' Martina Navratilova came "out of the closet," she followed on the path previously trod by Billie Jean King and Bill Tilden. The struggles and victories of athletes encourage their public in ways that politicians never could.

In that vein, baseball in particular was the field for many Americans' dreams for social inclusion in the twentieth century. For example, the Los Angeles Dodgers paved the way for integration on repeated occasions. Back in Brooklyn, general manager Branch Rickey made history in 1945 when he signed African American shortstop Jackie Robinson from the Negro Leagues to a minor league contract. In 1947 Robinson broke the major's color barrier that stood for sixty years. Soon came the battery of Roy Campanella and Don Newcombe in 1949, and pitcher Joe Black, who was National League Rookie of the Year in 1952.

Historian Howard Zinn noted, "The most important thing [Robinson] did was to change the invisibility of racial segregation, not just in baseball but in all of society."[63] Basketball followed the lead of Robinson (who was an all-conference hoopster at UCLA) by overturning its unwritten rule of segregation. In 1950, Chuck Cooper, Earl Lloyd, and Nat "Sweetwater" Clifton were the first black players drafted into the NBA. However, as the first black coach in the NBA in 1966 (who refused his induction into the Hall of Fame in 1974), Bill Russell distinctly recalled the prejudice he encountered. For example, in 1958, his second year in the NBA, Russell was chosen MVP, "yet when the sportswriters voted, I was not even on the first All-NBA team. They had to trip all over themselves to leave me out, putting three white forwards on the team and no center at all."[64]

As Jim Brown and Ernie Davis were bowling down football barriers for the Cleveland Browns, Oscar Robertson was playing for his hometown Cincinnati Royals (the predecessor to the Sacramento Kings). The 6'5" point guard amazingly averaged a triple double for the entire 1961–62 season (over 30 points, 12 rebounds, and 11 assists), and over a five-year period from 1961 to 1965 (30 points, 10 rebounds, 10 assists). But looking back, Robertson emphasized that he needed a tough hide to survive. "I was raised in the ghetto. I couldn't go downtown to the theatre; I could hardly get on the bus unless I sat in the back. I couldn't use public toilet facilities. People don't understand that in life your future reflects on what you did in your past. But it's how you manage that future and forget about things that happen to you. You have to think about the positive and that's what I tried to do."[65] But neither Russell nor Robertson could have foreseen that in 2003, 90% of the NBA's players and almost 50% of its coaches would be black.

Meanwhile, America's pastime proceeded to make headlines on the international front. In 1981 Mexican Americans rejoiced as Los Angeles Dodgers pitcher Fernando Valenzuela came out of obscurity to win Rookie of the Year, the Cy Young, and the World Series (over the rival New York Yankees). Since the 1960s the Majors had tapped into Latin American bush leagues and national teams, and by the end of the 1999 season, nine out of the top ten hitters in the American League had Latino ancestry.[66]

Soon the Dodgers opened its clubhouse doors to Asia by signing two new pitchers, Korean Chan Ho Park in 1994 and Japanese Hideo Nomo, who became Rookie of the Year in 1995. Nomo's triumphs suddenly made Japan's baseball league the fashionable source for new talent. In 2001, the Seattle Mariners hired stellar outfielder Ichiro Suzuki, and in 2003 the New York Yankees cherry-picked slugger Hideki Matsui (nicknamed "Godzilla"), the latest addition to about twenty Asian players in the big leagues.

After the amazing success story of the preternatural and multi-ethnic Tiger Woods (whose mother is Thai), the wave engulfed women's golf. In 1998, one South Korean woman played on the Ladies Professional Golf Association (LPGA) tour. Now they comprise half of the top thirty money winners, and the "Seoul Sisters" Se Ri Pak, Mi-Hyun Kim, and Grace Park have risen to the top six. With Hyundai's sponsorship, the tournament leaderboards are often displayed in both English and Korean.[67] Eighteen-year-old Korean American golfer Alice Kim said, "Once Se Ri started to hit the scene and become a little more popular, that's when a lot of the Korean girls started to pick it up. That was the big rush for Asian girls."[68] At the LPGA's 2003 US Open, fourteen of the 156 players were teenagers, and ten of them were of Korean descent. Looking for the next girl wonder, golf has shone the spotlight on the 13-year-old, six-foot-tall Michelle Wie. The youngest winner ever of a US Golf Association event (founded in 1884), Wie stated, "I don't want to be normal. I want to be something else."[69]

Basketball is finally catching up. Formerly a New York Knicks guard, ESPN analyst Greg Anthony made the connection with Yao: "His cultural significance can never be downplayed.... For China, it's up there with what happened with Jackie Robinson. You have to put it in that context. As much as the phenomenon has grown here, I still don't think we have an appreciation of what [impact] he has had in his homeland.... Much like Jackie Robinson was the right person, this guy is really the right person because he is such a classy person and he has such a great demeanor."[70]

The comparison to Jackie Robinson isn't exact. Sixty years ago, the US had legalized racial segregation with Jim Crow laws that were gradually eliminated in the momentous struggle for civil rights, culminating in the landmark 1954 Supreme Court decision on *Brown v. Board of Education*, The Civil Rights Act of 1964, and the Voting Rights Act of 1965. But Yao is helping to break down color lines and empower his Asian American supporters in the process. US ambassador to China from 1996 to 1999, James Sasser said of the comparison to Robinson, "I think it's somewhat similar. Jackie Robinson was breaking racial barriers. It's a little more complicated than that for Yao. I think he carries the responsibility of the Chinese race. He also carries the responsibility of showing that the Chinese can compete

THE TAO OF YAO

effectively, not necessarily against Americans but as part of this society. He carries the banner of the Chinese people."[71]

Professor Bob Wang, the director of the Chinese-American Business Institute at Fairleigh Dickinson University, summarized Yao's impact:

> Basketball is the fastest growing sport in the world, and Yao Ming coming to play in America could bring together two great powers faster than any political negotiating. It will bring China into America and give huge numbers of Chinese-Americans somebody who can incorporate them into the mainstream of US society. Added to that, he will have 10,000 fans banging down the doors to see their hero whenever he plays in New York, San Francisco or Los Angeles.[72]

Yao noticed their presence: "One thing I've found in every place I've been to in America, there's some Chinese people."[73] Immediately Yao inspired websites devoted to chronicling his every move (www.yaomingmania.com) and burgeoning fan clubs that take pride in attending his games en masse. President of Houston's www.yaomingfanclub.org, Michael Chang, said, "I know wherever he goes, attendance goes up. Chinese people who may have never cared about basketball come to see him."[74] Once Yao suited up, Asian fans did make their voices heard, voting with their feet and their wallets. Overnight the Houston Rockets' group ticket sales to Asian organizations jumped from 1% to 12%.[75]

Mapping his road to success in America, Yao said, "Everything will be based on my own hard work. Chinese people have a saying that to be successful there are two things you need. One is hard work, and the other is a little bit of luck."[76] Through this simple comment, generations of Asian Americans immediately could identify with and root for this lanky newcomer.

The ideal of the American Dream has long attracted Chinese immigrants. Many of the first Chinese came to California to strike it rich in the Gold Rush in 1849. Those who returned home spread tales of the "Gold Mountain" and convinced scores of their countrymen that they too could strike it rich if their persistent toil and good fortune paid off.

This saga of Chinese Americans has long fascinated the distinguished journalist Bill Moyers. Consequently, Moyers produced and hosted the three-part television series *Becoming American: The Chinese Experience*, which aired on PBS in the spring of 2003. "Chinese Americans—and recent arrivals—grapple with the issues that every immigrant group has had to face over time," elaborated Moyers. "What does it mean to become American? What do you give up when you become American if you're an immigrant? What traditions do you try to preserve? This question, and others, lie at the very heart of our democracy—past and present."

Recounting American history, warts and all, the series covered how the US Congress passed the infamous Chinese Exclusion Act in 1882, which reversed America's immigration policy. Moyers interviewed historian L. Ling-chi Wang, who traced the backlash of racism against Chinese Americans: "Up until 1882 America was open to everybody who wanted to come. We welcomed everybody. The only people that we excluded by law, at that time, were prostitutes, lepers, and morons, and in 1882 we added the Chinese to that list," said Wang. Moyers saw the cycle come full circle eighty years later. As the White House's Press Secretary, right in front of the Statue of Liberty he watched President Lyndon Johnson sign the Immigration and Naturalization Act of 1965, which rescinded these discriminatory racial quotas.

Making it to and in America has always been a difficult row to hoe. The Chinese were the unacknowledged laborers who constructed the transcontinental railroad in the nineteenth century. They were the unappreciated residents who fought for citizenship and equal treatment under the law in the twentieth century. They have been the undeterred asylum seekers who hide in suffocating shipping containers to cross America's borders in the twenty-first century. With the odds stacked against them, Chinese Americans have prioritized the concept of "saving face"—to preserve self-respect and avoid controversy, to maintain composure in the face of animosity. To soldier on, be good examples, and pave the way for others to follow more easily.

Unsurprisingly, Yao behaves in the same way, saying, "I hope I am a good textbook. It seems to me I am here to do more than play basketball. You have to understand that in China there is a lot of emphasis on collective honor and the honor of the entire country. I'd like Americans to see how Chinese people really work hard in difficult situations. I hope that, through my work in the NBA, they can see that."[77]

Though presently constituting 5% of the overall population, Asians are one of the fastest-growing US ethnic groups (up nearly 68% since 1990). Of this pie, the Chinese are the largest slice, comprising more than 20% of nearly 13 million Asian Americans.[78] Noting that by 2050, Asians may account for one out of every ten Americans, Professor Warren Cohen from the University of Maryland has called the current era "the Asian American Century," as opposed to the so-called "American Century" of the 1900s. In his 2002 book by that title he writes:

> As we begin the twenty-first century, the United States, its people, and their culture cannot be considered products exclusively of Western civilization. The extensive— and intensive—contact with East Asia in the previous hundred or so years has changed America dramatically. Even if Asians stop coming to our shores, even if those already here were to assimilate at approximately the same rate and to the same extent as the Europeans who came before them, the integration of Asian culture with American culture could not be undone easily … the Asians among us and our contacts with Asia have led us to change our ideas about what constitutes art, what is edible, what an American looks like—our habits, values, and even our identity.[79]

A case in point is the growing trend of US families adopting Chinese infants. As a byproduct of China's strict one-child-per-family policy, parents who approved of the patriarchal custom of prizing male heirs and caretakers began abandoning their female offspring at an alarming rate. Consequently in 2002 there were more than 5,000 successful

THE TAO OF YAO

placements in the US, a number that grew over 1,400% in the past decade. Fascinatingly, as more Americans have adopted Chinese babies, they have intentionally embraced Chinese culture, incorporating its holidays, language, and cuisine into their daily lives. In Wauwatosa, Wisconsin, an adoptive mother of two girls, Pamela Downing, said, "Our Chinese-American identity is much stronger than our hodge-podge European ethnicity." In Hollywood, California, a father named Cary Berger who is adopting a second daughter said, "I feel presumptuous saying we're Chinese-American. But with the number of girls coming into the country, there will have to be a way to describe us that takes less than five words."[80]

On other fronts as Asian Americans attain more academic, professional, and financial success, they become more assertive of their political and economic clout. Notable examples include Washington Governor Gary Locke, Hawaiian US Senators Daniel Inouye and Daniel Akaka, and Presidential Cabinet members Secretary of Transportation Norm Mineta and Secretary of Labor Elaine Chao. But in the realm of cultural celebrity, Yao instantly became Asian Americans' highest-profile standard-bearer. Like the legendary kung fu pioneer Bruce Lee thirty years before him, Yao galvanized the public's imagination. Cheering for his aspirations, admiration, and acceptance was the same as their own. That is why Asians soon reacted so strongly to Shaq's controversial confrontation with Yao (but again, more on that later).

Across the country, NBA teams were quick to cater to this "new" basketball demographic. Welcoming Yao into town, the Boston Celtics festooned the Fleet Center with red Chinese flags and banners on "Asian-American night" and trotted out an Asian a cappella group to sing the national anthem, as well as Asian drummers and lion dancers to strut their stuff at halftime.[81] Other teams across the country followed suit with similar festivities whenever Yao came to visit.

Aware of the groundswell of support from Asian Americans everywhere he played, Yao reflected near the end of his first NBA season, "I'm pretty used to it by now. Every fan of mine is important to me."[82] Certainly, Yao learned that he could not afford to take any support for granted when his success in America was already nothing short of miraculous, just as his countrymen found a century before him.

THE TAO OF YAO

Chapter 5

The Rookie

A tree that can fill the span of a man's arms grows from a downy tip; a terrace nine stories high rises from handfuls of earth.[1]
—Lao Tzu

A rookie has to do what a rookie has to do.[2]
—Yao Ming

Even before he got drafted, Yao became a lightning rod for criticism. Pundits were eager to prove their wisdom by loving him or hating him. Viewers have come to expect off-the-wall opinions from sportscaster Dick Vitale. However, in this case, Vitale forewarned:

I still feel that Yao Ming could be the second coming of LaRue Martin, the big man who was a first-round bust of the Portland Trail Blazers in 1972.... My gut feeling tells me the Rockets are making a mistake, baby, in evaluating their overall No. 1 pick. Still, Rudy T could shock America by having NBA commissioner David Stern announce [Duke guard Jay] Williams' name as the top pick. Then Houston would be moving toward the winner's circle.[3]

Jumping on the bandwagon, Mel Daniels, Indiana Pacers director of player personnel, belittled Yao's professional prospects: "He doesn't have the things that are necessary for him to frighten people. I'm from the old school. You have to have people in the post who pose a threat. Alonzo Mourning poses a threat to you when you come in the paint. This young man might serve you tea."[4]

Others came to Yao's defense. The 1991 NBA Executive of the Year (while with Portland), Bucky Buckwalter was a true trailblazer who scoured both the US and abroad for budding talent. As described by writer David Halberstam a decade earlier, this former 6'4" player "was a ubiquitous figure in professional basketball. He had been everywhere and done everything, scouted, served as agent, coached in the colleges, coached in the pros; he seemed to have held every conceivable job in basketball, save that of commissioner." Assisting coach Jack Ramsey, Buckwalter helped pick up the pieces after Walton's abrupt departure following the Blazers' 1977 championship season. According to Halberstam, back then Buckwalter already had pioneered the active recruitment of black players in America's South:

Given the number of superb black athletes in the country, how much greater their educational opportunities

---

"In life, we must begin to give a public performance before we have acquired even a novice's skill; and often our moments of seeming mastery are upset by new demands, for which we have acquired no preparatory facility."[5]

—Lewis Mumford

were becoming, it was undoubtedly the first wave of something large. The sport, [Buckwalter] sensed, was about to change color. Watching that game he realized that all the coaching rules of the past, so carefully drilled into players like him—where to set your body, where to position your feet—were meaningless. Those rules were for a slow game played on the floor by slow players and this was a new acrobatic game where players floated above the floor.

He decided that he wanted to be a link between the old world of basketball and the new world of basketball.[6]

Scarcely a decade later, Buckwalter wanted to catch the next wave—the recruiting of international players. Back in the 1986–87 draft, most of his peers thought Buckwalter wasted his #24 pick by selecting center Arvydas Sabonis in the first round. Though long desired by NBA scouts for his prowess in the Olympics, Sabonis was considered a lost cause since the USSR still kept him under lock and key. But then Mikhail Gorbachev became Soviet premier and enacted his revolutionary new policy of "glasnost" (openness) and "perestroika" (reform). After the fall of the Iron Curtain, Buckwalter's gamble in the future paid off. In 1995 Sabonis signed with Portland and paid them dividends up until his retirement at the end of the 2002–03 season. Now regarding Yao, Buckwalter said:

He is an outstanding young man. He's not just 7-5 but a talented, active athlete, and the guy is mentally tough. He has great ambition to succeed in the NBA, and he is going to. It will take a year, but he will make an impression early on. His biggest strength is shot-blocking, but he is a great passer, too. Reminds me of Sabonis, and, at 7-5, he can see over people. He locates and gets the ball to people at the right time. He speaks decent English, so there will be no problem coaching him. Eventually, he will become the best big man ever to play in the NBA.[7]

This time Bucky wasn't a lonely voice in the wilderness. Former Indiana Pacers head coach Isiah Thomas was used to playing among the trees. Playing for Bobby Knight's Indiana Hoosiers, the 6'1", 185-lb point guard won the NCAA championship in 1981. Drafted by the Detroit Pistons, he became the 1982 Rookie of the Year, an All-Star point guard, back-to-back NBA champion (1989–90), and one of only four players with 9,000 career assists (along with John Stockton, Magic Johnson, and Oscar Robertson). Thomas said of Yao, "I think he's going to be a phenomenal player. I think he's got all the skills. It's just a matter of him getting used to the league. He's got everything that you want a big guy to have. I've never seen a man that large with that type of athleticism and skill."[8]

But regardless of all the postulating, one thing was clear before the 2002–03 season even started. Yao would still be a rookie.

Try as he might to blend in with the crowd, he would have to suffer the petty and humiliating chores that veteran players foist upon naïve NBA freshmen. Since time immemorial, the hazing of newcomers has been a ritual of acceptance into a clan, surviving today in the form of college freshmen who rush fraternities, for example, and military recruits in basic training (infamously depicted at South Carolina's The Citadel in Pat Conroy's book and movie *The Lords of Discipline* and in real life by cadet Shannon Faulkner). Kids dream their whole life about getting into a club, but many don't consider that staying a member may be even harder. NBA rookies endure a similar rite of passage. Rockets scorer Glen Rice owned up to how the old hands planned to test Yao: "We're going to work him hard in practice, and we're going to work him hard carrying bags. He can be 8-foot-9, and we're still going to give him the rookie treatment. We can hang a lot of bags on him."[9]

No one was immune from this custom. At 6'9" and 255 lbs, Magic Johnson revolutionized the position of point guard. MVP three times in the regular season as well as in the five championships he won, Magic was also MVP in two of his twelve All-Star games. After leading Michigan State to defeat Larry Bird's Indiana State in the NCAA title game, Magic Johnson was the #1 pick of the 1979 draft. But his Laker teammates still stuck him with menial tasks. Nicknamed "Buck" for resembling a "young buck," Magic remembered how he was told to serve their particularly ornery captain. "I was Kareem's rookie all through that first year," he writes. "Whenever we were at the airport, he would ask me to pick him up a hot dog and nachos ... when you're a rookie, one job quickly leads to another. When the other guys see you going over to that dog stand, you might as well get out your pencil and start taking orders."[10]

There were legitimate concerns over how Yao would

handle the transition. After being drafted Yao acknowledged the worry. "It took me two years to adapt to going from my club team to the national team. This is a lot different. When I was selected to play for the national team, there was not that much attention focused on me in 1998. Now, everybody is giving me advice; everybody is wanting to talk to me. I'm under the microscope."[11]

People questioned Yao's preparation, since he would go from one treadmill to the next. First he would play in the FIBA 2002 World Basketball Championships held from August 29 to September 8, 2002, in Indianapolis, Indiana. China finished a disappointing twelfth among sixteen teams with a dreadful 1–7 record, though Yao was named center on the all-tournament team (in just 28 minutes per game, he averaged 21 points, 9 rebounds, and 2 blocks and shot 75% from the floor). Second, he was committed to play for China in the Asian Games in South Korea from September 29 to October 14, 2002 (China lost to South Korea in the finals, despite Yao's 23 points and 22 rebounds). Third, he would jump into the NBA without a breather. At that point Yao summarized, "I have missed a month of pre-season training due to national duties. I hope I could get used to the NBA play in ten games."[12]

Consequently, some speculated whether Yao would wilt over the course of the NBA season. Undeniably it was a marathon of non-stop travel, almost three times longer than the Chinese basketball league's. But this troubles all college players, since the NCAA basketball season is rarely more than thirty games. Magic Johnson said, "One of the hardest things for a rookie to get used to is the incredibly long and draining NBA season.... The travel and the schedule take their toll on you, and by the middle of January most rookies are ready for their summer vacation."[13]

But despite his taxing pre-existing obligations, Yao confirmed that he was in it for the long haul: "I need to work on my weight training and speed. My stamina is getting better but it's also something that needs to be better.... The NBA season is 82 games in six months so that will be hard for me. But I think this is a good preparation for me."[14]

But if it weren't, Yao had nowhere to hide. He was also one of just three Chinese players in the NBA, and the last of the "Walking Great Wall" trio to arrive. In 2000–01, 7'1" CBA All-Star and MVP Wang Zhi Zhi was the first by joining the Dallas Mavericks, and 6'11" Mengke Bateer followed when he signed with the Denver Nuggets. But because Yao was #1 draft pick and one of the tallest players on the planet, the expectations on him were much steeper.

Finally Yao joined the Rockets at the tail end of the preseason. He was just in time to have an underwhelming debut against the San Antonio Spurs. Wrestling against the tag team of 7'0" 250-lb Tim Duncan and 7'1" 250-lb David Robinson was no picnic. Yao quipped since, "They left a very deep impression on me." Then Yao addressed the difference between perception and reality: "When you watch on TV it seems easy. When you're out there playing, it is really difficult. The NBA is not something everybody can do. I felt like a rookie." On a lighter note, Robinson smiled, "There haven't been too many guys in this league who made me feel short. There's been one or two. Wow, he's big."[15]

His coach was compassionate. "To get those first-game

jitters out of the way was great," suggested Rudy Tomjanovich. "It's just something you've got to go through. I remember the first time I got in the game. I shot my first shot from the free throw line. It didn't hit the rim. I got the rebound at the free throw line. That's how hard I shot it."[16]

The officiating was another matter. Like all referees, NBA zebras are accused of having a double standard. Favoritism for the league's luminaries was once called "The Jordan Rules" in honor of the preferential treatment given to MJ. Yao was now in the unaccustomed position of being on the short end. "The reffing is something I can't control. I could have played better; but there are some rules I have to get used to," he noted.[17] One of the 50 Greatest Players in NBA History, 1992 Olympic gold medallist, and 2002 Hall of Famer, Magic Johnson has been there before: "The officials will never admit it, but every rookie has to pay his dues, just as every star gets a few breaks. When you've got a veteran who makes great moves and excites the fans, the refs go easy on him. After all, nobody pays good money to see Michael Jordan or Larry Bird foul out. By my third year in the league I was making some of the same defensive plays that had gotten me into trouble when I was a rookie, but now I was getting away with them."[18]

A few weeks into his rookie year, Yao again addressed his lack of standard preparation. "I've missed out on a lot of opportunities. I've missed preseason games, preseason practices, so it's been tough. I don't think there are any other first-year players that have had to do that."[19] By recognizing that he started at the bottom of the totem pole instead of its top, Yao ensured that if he exceeded people's current expectations, he would come out far ahead in the future. But by that time, his peers would lend their support.

One was Vlade Divac. The 7'1" center for the Sacramento Kings, he was one of the first stars to make the leap from Europe to America. Back then Jerry West was searching for a worthy successor to Kareem Abdul-Jabbar, who would soon retire. Impressed by Divac, who helped the Yugoslavian national team win an Olympic silver medal in 1988, West made him the #26 pick in the 1989 NBA draft. Divac rewarded the Lakers by earning a spot on the NBA All-Rookie Team and becoming a consistent contributor. But Divac didn't forget about his native land. Even after it had descended into a bitter civil war, Divac returned to win Yugoslavia another silver in the 1996 Olympics. However, then West made a more momentous move: he traded Divac to the Charlotte Hornets for the draft rights for a cocky Pennsylvania high schooler who was turning pro, and then applied the leftover money to land a colossal free agent with a $120 million contract for seven years.[20] Kobe Bryant and Shaquille O'Neal would soon establish another dynasty in the City of Angels.

Stung by the trade, Divac overcame this setback to finally become an All-Star in 2001. His reputation was secure abroad, for as Divac acknowledged, "I am Michael Jordan in Yugoslavia."[21] Now Divac empathized with Yao: "I can

---

"For him, I think it's very important how [the Rockets] adopt him. I was ▶ lucky. The whole Lakers organization helped me a lot. Hopefully, the Rockets are doing the same for him."[22]

—Vlade Divac

relate to what he's going through. It has been a long time since I came here. But I remember there were a lot of difficulties. First, the language and then the system. And not just international guys, but you see in a lot of rookies, they are not consistent. And his game is the same way. But he's going to be a great player."[23]

Another admirer was Dirk Nowitzki, a 7'0", 240-lb slasher as deadly from the three-point line as when skying above the rim. Drafted by the Milwaukee Bucks in 1998 from the DJK Wurzburg team of the German Bundesliga league, Nowitzki was a prodigy. He had played on the 1996 German National Junior Team, German Under-22 National Team, European Junior Select Team, and the World Junior Select Team. Used to being the "go to" guy, Nowitzki was in for a rude awakening in the NBA. Sitting on the pine was an uncomfortable sensation for him, as he had to bide his time before emerging as a bona-fide superstar:

> My first year, there were games I didn't play at all. In Germany, I was the man. I played 40 minutes, scored whenever I wanted. To come over to a totally new situation, to be a nobody . . . it was tough. But I had a great coaching staff and great teammates that supported me. That was huge. You just have to take it. The rookie season is going to be up and down, no matter how old you are, or where you're from. It's going to be tough. [Yao] just has to believe in himself and work hard, try to get better every day. Once he does that, the sky is the limit for him.[24]

THE TAO OF YAO

Midway through the year when questioned about his inconsistent play, Yao replied, "First, I am a rookie. It is normal for a rookie to encounter such a problem, and it is also my first time having such a problem. Sometimes even myself, I don't know the exact reason. What I can say is that I could not find my rhythm and feel on the court. Also, maybe I have not played against so many strong players before. Please keep on watching me play. This is my first NBA season, and I think it is normal to face such problems."[25]

Former NBA coach Jeff Van Gundy defended Yao as well: "He's going through things that no first-round pick has ever gone through. He didn't get a chance to participate in the summer league, no workouts in the fall, no first weeks of training camp, doesn't speak the language or have a basis in the culture. So he's trying to assimilate in so many important areas."[26]

As the season moved onward, Yao would prove that he did think and perform differently than a typical first-year player. Rudy Tomjanovich concluded, "He's easy to communicate with. A lot of rookies, you're talking a foreign language to them anyway. There are two different sports: college basketball and pro basketball."[27] But even when headed to the fabled All-Star game, Yao didn't want to be treated differently or singled out: "I feel like the rookies are my brothers."[28] Deferentially he downplayed the fanfare: "I still believe that I am a blue-collar, a blue-collar amongst the All-Stars."[29]

Just like a sword is tempered by numerous dips into the flame, Yao experienced a series of trials by fire. Besides, who could have expected to be grilled on national television by the indefatigable Charles Barkley and emerge with his credibility better than it was before?

The Bite of Charles Barkley

When you are content to be simply yourself and don't compare or compete, everybody will respect you.[30]
—Lao Tzu

Respect is something you earn, not something someone gives to you.[31]
—Yao Ming

Charles Barkley's reputation for throwing his weight around has only grown since his transition from a hot-headed basketball player to a loose-lipped talking head. Or as he once put it, "I don't create controversies. They're there long before I open my mouth. I just bring them to your attention."

Drafted out of Auburn, this 6'5", 250-lb locomotive was nicknamed "the Round Mound of Rebound." He played first with the Philadelphia 76ers (itself languishing after "Doctor J" Julius Erving and Moses Malone led the team to the 1982 title) and then with Phoenix and Houston. When he retired in 2000, he was one of only four players who had amassed over 20,000 points, 10,000 rebounds, and 4,000 assists. Though he never managed to get a title ring, it wasn't because he didn't try. Bill Walton said, "Barkley is like Magic [Johnson] and Larry [Bird] in that they don't really play a position. He plays everything; he plays basketball. There is nobody who does what Barkley does. He's a dominant rebounder, a dominant defensive player, a three-point shooter,

◆ "Can't nobody on planet Earth guard me, no one. I mean that."

—Charles Barkley

a dribbler, a playmaker."[32] True to form, Barkley became an
All-Star for eleven straight years (1987–1997), league Most

Valuable Player in 1993, and a member of the NBA Top 50 players in 1996.

In his prime Barkley ran with the original "Dream Team" that included the living legends Larry Bird, Magic Johnson, and Michael Jordan and swept the 1992 Olympic Games. (Barkley would re-enlist to grab another gold in 1996.) Back then in Barcelona, Spain, Barkley uniquely advanced the cause of American basketball diplomacy. Before yet another one-sided blowout, Barkley said, "I don't know anything about Angola, but I know they're in trouble."[33] During a streak in the game when Team USA outscored its African counterpart 46–1, Barkley mixed it up under the basket and left his calling card by emphatically elbowing a hapless Angolan player in the chest. In front of a worldwide television audience, the image would be perceived as a superpower's act of hubris against a Third World country. After the 116–48 thrashing, Sir Charles explained, "Somebody hits me, I'm going to hit him back. Even if it does look like he hasn't eaten in a while." For the uninitiated, Barkley labeled the incident as a necessary act of self-defense—"a ghetto thing"— since "well, he might have pulled a spear on me." As they say, no blood, no foul.

However, even when he was still in China Yao freely admired this powder keg: "I have determination like Charles Barkley. Even if Barkley never won a championship, he never lost his fire to win one. I also like his slam-dunks."[34]

Now recently retired, Barkley enjoys the privilege of pontificating to a TV audience. Before the 2002 season began, Barkley renewed a $1.5 million-a-year contract with AOL Time Warner to keep shooting off his mouth on the

THE TAO OF YAO

TNT cable program *Inside the NBA* and CNN's *TalkBack Live*.[35] Remember, here's a guy who claimed he was misquoted in his own 1993 autobiography *Outrageous!*, and then went on to pen another book entitled *I May Be Wrong but I Doubt It*. Using the studio as his soapbox, he has relished skewering players and coaches alike, and viewers revel in his blustery banter.

It was just a matter of time before Barkley set his sights on the newest and biggest target in the land.

Barely two weeks into the 2002 season, Barkley lit into Yao. As the TNT cameras were rolling, commentator Kenny Smith compared Yao's early development to that of explosive 6'11" swingman Kevin Garnett from the Minnesota Timberwolves. As an aside, Garnett had played against 19-year-old Yao in the 2000 Olympics in Sydney. The result was another predictably lopsided US 119–72 victory. Having skipped college to turn pro, Garnett licked his chops by calling the youngster "Fresh meat." But after the game, Garnett concluded, "He's very good, very skilled. He's got a head start on some things. No disrespect, he'll get an opportunity and he'll get better at some things."[36] Now goaded by his co-host, Barkley couldn't restrain himself any longer:

Yao Ming makes Shawn Bradley look like Bill Russell. He might be a good player some day, but he is not ready.... He has been playing the game all these years. You know what he said when he got over here, "Whoa! These brothers are different over here. They are big and strong and they run and jump. Whoa! Even white guys can play over here." He's never seen a brother in China.

The black guys and white guys—they aren't like those China guys, they're a little bit different over here.

Then he proceeded to utter these famous last words: "If he ever gets 19 points in a game, I'll kiss Kenny's ass right here on TV."[37]

Initially, Yao misinterpreted the report to mean that Barkley threatened to kiss him: "When I heard him say that, I knew that the most I could score that night would be 18 points."[38] Later, Yao gauged the swipe more soberly: "It's a little strange to me that people pay attention to things outside the game, rather than the competition itself. But that's not to say it's not fun. . . . I knew that Charles and other people in the NBA like to joke around. I didn't think I would be the focus of the jokes so quickly."[39]

Little did Barkley know that he would promptly trip over his tongue. Just a few days later on November 17th, Yao helped the Rockets defeat the Shaqless LA Lakers. In his best game of the young season, Yao had a perfect shooting night with 9 field goals and two free throws to score 20 points. Suddenly, it was payback time.

Kenny Smith was no slouch himself in estimating hoops talent. He played nine NBA seasons, five with Olajuwon in Houston, where he was the starting point guard for their 1994 and 1995 titles, and remained Houston's career leader in three-point shooting accuracy. After winning the bet Smith crowed, "I make people pay their debts. Charles will pay his debt to society, no question about it. He will pay his debt, and it will be on camera. Charles goes to Las Vegas a lot. In Vegas, you can't leave the table until you pay your debts."[40] Upon further reflection, Smith wondered how he'd collect it, though:

> Even when I win, I lose. Him kissing me anywhere is kind of flagrant, so I've got to think of something else. First I thought of this. What if I had a picture of me, and he kissed the picture? But I couldn't get a picture of my whole body, so that wasn't good either. So I said, you know what? I had a doll [a toy action figure of himself], so he could kiss the Kenny Smith doll. But then I thought....[41]

On CNN's *TalkBack Live* program on November 20th, Barkley was taking it like a man: "I am going to pay up [Thursday] night. If you make a bet, you pay up. I just told Kenny to take a shower before the show. I made the bet and I'm going to stick by my word. Ugh."[42]

Well, it didn't take long for Smith to make up his mind. The next day, November 21, Smith made his move with host Ernie Johnson Jr. on TNT's basketball show *Stand Up!* Before their telecast of the Rockets game against the Dallas Mavericks, they led an oblivious donkey onto the set. Cornered, Charles exclaimed, "Hey, man, you're trying to humiliate me." But he soon faced the music: "You know what? I'm a man of my word."[43] Puckering up, he planted a kiss on the animal's posterior to the chagrin of all involved. After the hilarity, they sat back and watched Yao reach new highs in the Rockets' loss to the Mavs: Yao shot 10 for 12 from both the field and the foul line for a total of 30 points. His impressive performance prompted further debate by the TNT crew.

TNT play-by-play commentator Jeff Van Gundy, typically dour, was beside himself with joy. "I can see why everybody wanted this guy. This is my first time to see this guy play live. This is some show he's putting on."[44]

Taking things a step further, Smith predicted that Yao would become one of the world's top five players. Barkley barked back, "Not only will I kiss your ass if he [Yao] becomes one of the five best players in the world ... we're going to get REAL freaky in here if he becomes one of the five best players in the world."[45] But then he couldn't help but backpedal some more: "Kenny said that I said Yao Ming couldn't play, and that's inaccurate. You don't want the Chinese mad at you. They can fight. I thought he would be good. I just didn't think it would be this soon."[46]

A day later his Airness himself weighed in on the topic, after his Washington Wizards lost to Yao's Rockets. Said Michael Jordan, "He's for real. Look at that 30 and 16 [points and rebounds against Dallas]. Any time you can make Charles Barkley kiss an ass, that's a good thing. I just couldn't tell which one was the ass. Was it a four-legged ass or a two-legged ass? ... [Yao's] getting better and better."[47]

After the dust settled, Coach Rudy Tomjanovich was in a unique position to evaluate Yao's status, since he had coached Barkley in the forward's final two seasons in Houston.

That passion is what impressed me the most when I first saw [Yao] play for extended time at the World Championships. He carries it with him on the floor. ... You'll think I'm crazy on this one, but I think he's a lot like Charles Barkley. They both love to play the game, and

© The Sporting News

◆ "[Yao] says he understands me about 70 percent of the time. I don't know how he has done as well as he has done. The good news is he has a feel for the game and he gained respect from his teammates his very first practice, with some of the things he did, even the veteran guys. We really have put him in a tough situation. Everybody wants to form this guy to their own idea, and they are looking for this finished product. And in reality, this guy is a senior in college."[48]

—Rudy Tomjanovich

that's obvious when you watch them for just a few minutes. I remember one of the first times I went to Philadelphia as a scout and Charles was a kid. He was standing at the foul line near the end of a game for two big free throws. So he gets the ball, he dribbles it a couple of times, then he looks straight into the TV camera and winks and smiles. Then he made the shots.[49]

Barkley wouldn't feel guilty for long. He was far from alone in his public underestimation of Yao's potential. Eventually pundits far and wide claimed *mea culpa,* temporarily shamed by their brash predictions on Yao's imminent demise. Few believed that Yao could convert legions of naysayers into such ardent supporters so rapidly. Critics like ESPN's Bill Simmons announced his about-face:

After the Rockets drafted Yao Ming last summer, I wrote that he'd get dunked on more than a cup of coffee at Krispy Kreme. I called him a "disaster waiting to happen," even throwing in the portentous phrase "Mark my words." The lesson, as always? I'm an idiot. Forget about Yao's emergence as the most polished rookie big man since Brad Daugherty, or that he offers the first worthy challenge to Shaq since Hakeem was still The Dream. If you're a basketball fan, you love Yao Ming. He's a godsend, the best Chinese import since General Tso. And I thought he'd stink.[50]

NBA Hall of Famer Rick Barry didn't smell anything bad about Yao. Barry was the only man to lead the NCAA, American Basketball Association (ABA), and NBA in scoring; the 6'7" forward was originally drafted #2 in the first round by the ABA and became Rookie of the Year in 1965. The definitive scoring machine, Barry was an All-Star twelve times in his fourteen-year career, and the Golden State Warriors' MVP on their 1975 NBA championship team. Coincidentally, Barry finished his career with the Houston Rockets, when they had to replace Tomjanovich, who had suffered a career-threatening injury. Known for his iconoclastic underhanded style, he became the NBA's career leader in free-throw percentage. Barry never kept his pride or opinions a secret, and his initial estimation of Yao was no exception:

> I hate to say I told you so, but I really did. For two years, I have said that Yao Ming can flat-out play. At his size, he is the best player I have ever seen and I believe that he will leave a lasting mark on the NBA. So far, he has exhibited an exceptional shooting touch, instinctive passing ability and a mental approach to the game that will guarantee his success. The other skills necessary to be a major force at the center position will come with time. Write this down: Yao Ming will be the first of many big men from China to make an impact in the NBA.[51]

Bill Walton couldn't help but join the chorus: "Are people still wondering about Yao Ming? The rush to be the first to criticize can often lead to a stampede off a cliff. As Elvis says, 'Return to Sender.'"[52]

Or as a venerated sage once put it:

To know that you do not know is the best.
To pretend to know when you do not know is a disease.[53]
—Lao Tzu

Chapter 6

The Art of Traveling

A journey of a thousand miles must begin with a single step.[1]
—Lao Tzu

I think it will be impossible for me to get used to everything right away. Basketball in America is like a culture. It is like a foreigner learning a new language. It is difficult to learn foreign languages, and it will also be difficult for me to learn the culture for basketball here. It is always fun to adapt to a new environment.[2]
—Yao Ming

In baseball, the Major Leagues is called "the Show." The pros beckon bright lights and big cities, and they are the heavenly destinations that only a select few are able to reach. Likewise, the NBA is the holy grail of every schoolyard basketball player from Brooklyn to Beijing. Fortunately for Yao, he got off on the right foot, as his curiosity about his big adventure matched that of the fans concerning him.

During the 2002 World Basketball Championships in Indianapolis, Yao was eager to embark on his journey. "Mostly, I am curious," he said. "The pace of life is much faster [in the United States] than where I live in China."[3]

Aside from athletic challenges, his new life also afforded him the opportunity to indulge in unfamiliar and otherwise previously forbidden freedoms. When asked what would be his activities on his first day off as an NBA player, Yao replied: "Video games, fishing, and driving." Diving headfirst into his financial and personal independence, Yao reportedly spent $5,000 to outfit his Texas home with the latest video game equipment.[4]

Yao had to acclimate himself to a different style of play as well. Asked about his first encounter with basketball culture shock, Yao recalled Nike's summer camp:

> It was strange at first to see such passion and emotion in the game. When I went to America, I didn't like to dunk much. It's not the Chinese way.... In America, I'd get the ball near the basket, shoot a layup, and the coach would be saying, "Dunk the ball!" But I was used to laying it in. Finally, the coach said, "If you get the ball in close and don't dunk it, all of your teammates are going to have to run laps." But I couldn't help it. I was very accustomed to laying the ball in the basket. All of my teammates were running laps, begging me to dunk. Finally, after about a week and many laps, I began to dunk it every time.[5]

◀ "A solitary traveler whom we saw perambulating in the distance loomed like a giant."[6]

—Henry David Thoreau

On his return trip to America, it didn't take long for Yao to get adjusted to the slam-happy NBA. After watching Yao's jitters in his first NBA game, Rockets forward Maurice Taylor forecasted, "Once he starts dunking on people he'll relax."[7] Ironically, Yao would earn his first technical foul after he stuffed home a basket. Did the penalty fit the crime? "I just screamed as I was dunking. I didn't say anything. Not a word, just a shout," rationalized Yao. "Coach [Tomjanovich] told us at halftime that we have to get stronger mentally on the court, and we have to take every opponent seriously. It's kind of like when you're in a traffic jam. You have to keep pushing forward. You can't turn back."[8]

After being pointed in the right direction, Yao was ready to step on the gas. To the appreciation of the hometown audience who unfortunately was used to the gridlock created from suburban sprawl, Yao had automobiles on his brain. "Having to drive so much in traffic" posed the most difficult challenge to him; Yao noted that "the most important word I've learned is traffic."[9] Eager to hit the road, he was forced to bide his time, and like all prospective drivers, was relegated to practicing in a parking lot. "I am usually resting whenever I can get the chance. I also talked about getting my driver's license. I've been really busy and haven't had time to get that taken care of yet, but when I get a chance I would like to get it done soon. Just so many things to do."[10] There sure were. Even as his teammates were fearful of being driven by him, Yao soon grew to understand that it was not always fun being chauffeured around all the time either.

On the Road Again . . .

*A good traveler has no fixed plans
and is not intent upon arriving.*[11]

—Lao Tzu

A century ago, a seven-foot man would have probably found employment as a giant in the circus. Today in the big top of the NBA, the big man is just another breed of entertainer. Taking its cue from the 1980s "Showtime" Lakers, the NBA has transformed its games into dizzying extravaganzas that overwhelm the senses. A game where Yao's Rockets played the Golden State Warriors in Oakland, California, typified the neo-carnival atmosphere. A bevy of dancing girls clad in hip-hugging tights gyrated across the floor. Frenetic mascots and acrobats cartwheeled crazily across the baseline. Neon lights flashed and splashy billboards rotated like clockwork. Costumed clowns whipped the crowd into a frenzy for free pizza and cajoled them in contests for prizes galore (a befuddled child won a cell-phone contract). Air cannons and floor-mounted slingshots launched balled-up t-shirts far into the mezzanine. There never seemed a spare second for the fan to rest.

The same held true for the players. The long march of the NBA season effectively separates the men from the boys as much mentally as it does physically. Kids on the living room couch fantasize about making the highlight reel of the evening sportscast. But few comprehend and less are prepared for the daily grind of packing suitcases, shuttling to and from the airport, overcoming jet lag, studying Xs and

Os, and pacing for the horn to sound.

Retiring in 1990 after a twenty-year career, Kareem Abdul-Jabbar had nearly every record that mattered. 38,387 points. 3,189 blocked shots. Six MVP Awards. Nineteen All-Star games. His first NBA title came with the Milwaukee Bucks in 1971, and he grabbed five more in Tinseltown. But Kareem took extra pride in surviving the rigors of the road, saying in his autobiography, "The demands of travel have expanded exponentially with the near doubling of the teams and the territory. [Lakers team physician] Doc Kerlan says the road schedule in the NBA would kill the average human being. He emphasizes the tremendous stress of this kind of traveling on the body, and the even greater stress on the mind. No other major sport has its players travel the way we do."[12]

The NBA is the latest greatest show on Earth, employing a band of wandering minstrels to amuse audiences from town to town. For them touring is a double-edged sword. On one hand, sightseeing can still be fun for a tourist at heart. Crisscrossing the country, pros have access to a world and its privileges that others never get to sample. Yao for one was still bright-eyed and bushy-tailed. Visiting the Supersonics in Seattle, he lamented, "I'm a little disappointed. I thought there would be a Starbucks on the bench."[13]

Later Yao could've used the jolt of caffeine. Spending more time sitting than shooting, Yao found coping with the wear and tear of life on the road hard indeed: "Everything is happening too rapidly, too fast."[14] Abruptly he found himself in the real-life version of the movies *Planes, Trains, and Automobiles* meets *Groundhog Day*. Hopping from one mode of transportation to the next is an unavoidable part of his job. If you thought the hefty actor John Candy had a hard time squeezing into his coach seat, just imagine Yao's predicament. As his teammate Steve Francis noted, "Even my Hummer is too small for him."[15]

Waking up every night in a different city, hotel room, and bed proved more taxing than it might seem (even though a New York hotel went to great lengths to accommodate Yao by attaching a twin bed to the foot of the king-size mattress in his room).[16] As soon as he got used to the pace of NBA play, Yao hit the wall from the grueling schedule of getting from one city to the next. He was tired of being tired, and tired of being asked how tired he was.

> I feel a lot better about the speed [of the game]. A lot better on both sides.... I'm very tired. Definitely, I think I'm not used to it yet. [In China] we went to at the most two or three cities on a trip.... I feel the pressure is more on me than other rookies. That makes everything harder. I definitely think the travel is different. It just makes me tired.[17]

> I did see the new Harry Potter movie recently while we were on the road. I liked it but it was a little long. It helps to have some free time when I'm on the road because traveling is very tiring. I feel very tired a lot of times.[18]

> I've never been through something like this before. I don't know if this is what you'd call tired or not. It's like if you've never been drunk before and get drunk for the

first time, you don't know that you're drunk. But I'm definitely pretty exhausted in some games.[19]

Even having just two days off at Christmas was nice. But you have to understand that if you give me one day to rest I want two days. If you give me two days I want three. Sometimes I feel like a tire that hasn't had air put in it for a long time.[20]

Aching for some much-needed rest, Yao was living these words written long ago:

The further one travels the less one knows.[21]
—Lao Tzu

Rick Adelman has been around the league for a long time, having spent fourteen years with the Portland Trail Blazers on three different occasions. The team's first captain in 1970, he returned to the Blazers as coach in 1989, leading them to the NBA finals twice. Therefore Adelman admired Yao's doggedness: "I've watched him as the year's gone on, and he's got unlimited talent, not just skills, but the way he sees the game and the way he understands the game. The pressure he is under, I don't know how he's doing it."[22]

Asked how he coped with the pressure, Yao replied, "The best way to deal with it is sleeping."[23] Reflexively, writers took this as an off-the-cuff remark, and readers missed the kernel of truth in it. Bill Walton said that John Wooden gave exactly the same advice to his players: "He used to tell us that it was more important to sleep well two nights before a game than the night before. He said sleep was a cumulative thing, and there was no way the body could recharge itself with only one night's worth of rest. 'You've got to build up to an event,' he said. Who knows if any of it was true, but I believed him."[24]

Magic Johnson underscored that catching Zs is an absolute necessity, writing, "That was another thing I had to get used to as a rookie—taking an afternoon nap whenever I could. It's impossible to fall asleep right after a game, so you end up having a lot of late nights. But there are always morning practices, or early wake-up calls, so you can get on the bus to the airport and fly on to the next city. The only way to survive in the NBA is to learn to sleep in the afternoons."[25]

Buck had learned well from the Big Fella. Kareem Abdul-Jabbar adhered to the principle of conservation of energy. "Within this context, you are under the constant pressure to perform and to win—pressure from the fans, from the management, from your own high standards," wrote Kareem. "So part of your job becomes learning how to play the NBA as well as the ball game. You trudge through the season with as much consistency and equilibrium and snatched rest as you can muster, with the goal of arriving at the play-offs with your physical being and your intensity of desire intact."[26]

Coach Tomjanovich noted, "I'm sure he is tired. He's done a lot, on and off the court. He just needs to get his battery recharged." Teammate Steve Francis volunteered some guidance as well: "I did everything too. He just has to learn what his body can take. But we can't just go away from him. If he's done, we're finished."[27]

Perhaps Yao could take comfort in the words of the wise:

Yield, and become whole.
Bend, and become straight.
Hollow out, and become filled.
Exhaust, and become renewed.[28]

—Lao Tzu

Just as the mythic phoenix rises from the ashes and is reborn, so does an individual's cycle of energy eventually renew itself. In due course, Yao would catch his second wind and finish the season holding his head high. As the regular season drew to a close, Yao tried to keep his focus. "We all love to play basketball. We're professional basketball players," he said. "I think that we can get through the weariness because of our love of basketball."[29]

But Yao loved other things as well, such as his family and homeland, and he would need to find a suitable replacement for both in his new digs deep in the heart of Texas.

Family Ties

I have three treasures which I possess and maintain securely.
The first is parental love.
The second is frugality.
The third is not daring to be first.[30]

—Lao Tzu

Yao grew used to fielding dumb questions as well as misunderstandings when reporters read too much into things. A case in point was when Yao answered, "Some people have asked me questions about the arm band I wore in the Philly game. No, it wasn't a fashion statement, I have a long scrape on my arm, so I had to cover it up. The cut is healing so after it heals, I will not be wearing it anymore."[31]

However, there was a reason why he regularly wore a red string bracelet on his wrist. It was part of a pair. Its mate was worn by Ye Li, a member of the Chinese women's national basketball team. Normally game to talk on any subject, Yao pursed his lips when her name came up. Asked about his relationship with his 6'3" girlfriend, Yao tersely replied, "This is a private matter. I refuse to answer."[32]

Tomjanovich also wore a band around his wrist. His rubber band reminded him that he could bounce back after bad situations. He had rebounded from many hardships—growing up poor, on welfare, with an alcoholic father. After a building a storied basketball career, he nearly died from being punched in a freak accident with Kermit Washington on December 9, 1977. Against all odds, he came back to play again more than respectably. Then his greatest moments lay ahead as he guided the team to twin titles. But in the aftermath, he plumbed his dignity to admit that he suffered from alcoholism himself and needed help. "I just snap the rubber band to remind myself, 'Hey, it's okay. I have a great life going here, and if something goes wrong I can handle it.' That's the difference now, I know I can handle things. I feel great not only about my life, but about myself."[33]

Yao had to tackle his own uncomfortable self-examination. It was inevitable that Yao would catch a case of homesickness. Thrust into a foreign land, anyone could become disoriented and lonely. Unsurprisingly, Yao expressed such sentiments: "I miss a kind of atmosphere, a kind of familiar atmosphere when I'm not in the gym. Nothing [here] is familiar besides the gym."[34] At a press conference before the All-Star game, Yao wore his Chinese national team jersey because, "I just want my teammates to know that I miss my audience and friends back in China."[35] Later he would add, "Leaving home is hard to express. I miss everything."[36]

But despite the nostalgia, Houston was where he'd live for the foreseeable future. Ironically, Yao's replacement on his hometown team simultaneously faced the reverse culture shock. The Shanghai Sharks hired Dan McClintock, a 7'0" journeyman center from Visalia, California, and charged him with the unenviable task of filling Yao's size-18 shoes. So it was up to Yao to make the best of it in the wild west.

Little did Yao know that his coach had once been in a similar situation. Tomjanovich and his wife Sophie had grown to like San Diego in his rookie year with the Rockets. But when the team changed ownership and moved to the Lone Star State, he had no choice but to pack his bags and head east. There the Houston climate shocked his system. "I think we were sick the entire first month we were there," recalled Tomjanovich. "You go from a hundred degrees outside to fifty degrees with air-conditioning blasting inside everywhere. You were bound to get sick. Between that and the fact that it rained every afternoon, we missed San Diego a lot."[37]

There was one thing that could make Yao's transition easier and help him recover between games. Here his government amazingly came to the rescue. Both his parents were cleared to leave China and live with their son. Thankful for this unexpected luxury, Yao returned the favor by dipping into his first paycheck to feather his nest for their arrival. No average souvenir-shopping tourist could measure up to Yao, who divulged that "the first thing I bought in America" was a four-bedroom house in Houston to accommodate his mom and dad.[38]

Yao owed a lot to his parents, especially his genes. His father, Yao Zhi Yuan, is 6'7". He played center in Shanghai and was a forward on the men's national team. His mother, Fang Feng Di, is 6'3" and was a member of the Chinese national women's team. But as she put it, Fang was unable to play in the Olympics "due to special historical circumstances in our country," otherwise known as Mao's Cultural Revolution.[39]

Growing up, Yao was grateful to his folks for giving him the space to stretch his wings: "They gave me freedom, not pressure. They gave me freedom to decide what I wanted to do. That was the most important part of my growth."[40] Although the roundball road that eventually led to the US was long and arduous, Yao affirmed it was his choice to embark upon it. "My parents didn't teach me basketball like it was a profession. They taught me for fun."[41]

As a good son, Yao knew how fortunate he was to be able to recreate his home away from home. "I am very blessed to have my mother and father with me," confirmed Yao. "It feels great to have a home to come back to every night."[42] A big part of the comfort zone was just having someone familiar to talk to. "My parents are doing well. My father just went back to China but he will be returning shortly. My mother is adjusting to life here, she is still not used to it. But she has friends here that keep her company and take her out, so it makes it easier for her to live here. I think it helps that I get to see and talk to her often."[43]

Listening to her maternal instincts, Fang Feng Di expressed concern about her only child:

I do see the pressure on him. And I hope that I can help, help him to relax. I worry. If he worries, I worry. If he's happy, I'm happy. We often talk about it at home. I want to give him support. I want to be able to provide a place where he can feel at home, so that when he has worries outside, when he comes back, he has something to rely on. I think a good mother and a good father can do that. I worry about him. I see the pressure. I worry.[44]

Another member of Yao's inner circle saw this dynamic too. His interpreter Colin Pine appreciated how the presence of parents made a world of difference to Yao. "He is not very different at home. But he can let his guard down. I really don't see the pressure showing on him. I'm consistently amazed with how well he deals with the pressure. His mother is able to sense what is going on. I think it's the same as with anybody. It's a home. You get home and kind of forget about a lot of things you deal with on the outside."[45]

Another benefit of having his parents around was the home cooking. At the start of his journey Yao observed, "I think it's probably more difficult for me to adjust to the diet than the language."[46] Eating well would refuel his spirit, as

Yao ticked off: "Pork chops, chicken soup and anything that my mother cooks are my favorite foods."[47] However, dining out was another matter, as Yao disclosed: "I try to eat a lot of Chinese food. Up until yesterday, I've been able to eat my mother's cooking almost every day. Obviously when I'm on the road, I can't eat my mother's cooking, because my interpreter can't cook."[48]

As Thanksgiving approached, the press peppered Yao about his thoughts on the holiday. As a modern-day Pilgrim in a new world, he mused on what this American tradition meant to him:

> I have heard of the turkey that is at the center of this meal. I have tasted some of it before, maybe sliced up or in pieces. But I have never seen a whole turkey served for a meal. And I have definitely never eaten a whole turkey.... I have been hearing people talk about the holiday as it has gotten closer. I am looking forward very much to having the experience.... You tell me about all of these things that we will have, so maybe I will decide not to eat all day until we sit down for the dinner.... In ancient Chinese culture, there was always a celebration at the time when the fields were first sown, a prayer that the crops would grow. Today, the tradition continues among people who do farming. There are other times when all of us stop to give thanks for what we have. I'll find it interesting to see the American side of this.... Now I am most looking forward to eating some turkey, learning about America.[49]

Later he would merely confess, "I don't really enjoy eating turkey, I prefer KFC."[50] Although this response was comical, it was less surprising than it might seem. In China, Kentucky Fried Chicken rakes in $250 million in annual revenues with more than six hundred locations. There, consistent quality and cleanliness alone make a restaurant noteworthy. Furthermore, the multinational chain has adapted to local tastes by serving Peking Duck and featuring the baseball-capped chicken "QiQi" instead of the southern grandfather Colonel Sanders.[51] Now in America, Yao was even more receptive to fast food. "His mom's a wonderful cook," his traveling companion Pine allowed. "But Yao likes pizza and chicken wings."[52]

Local Hospitality

Thus the Master travels all day
without leaving home.
However splendid the views,
he stays serenely in himself.[53]

—Lao Tzu

Even though he was a stranger in a strange land, Yao went out of his way to pay the proper respect to those in positions of authority. As Christmastime rolled around, Yao mailed a greeting card to Shaq's father Philip "Sarge" Hamilton, who first expressed disbelief and then sought Yao out to get an autograph in person. But that was the tip of the iceberg. As *ESPN The Magazine* recounted, Yao also gave a holiday greeting "to every center he faced before Christmas, to every GM who attended his predraft workout in Chicago last May, and to Michael Jordan. He personally handed cards to the Rockets front office staff and bought gifts for Tomjanovich, GM Carroll Dawson, and Michael Goldberg, the team counsel who helped negotiate clearance with the Chinese Basketball Association and the Shanghai Sharks to play here. 'First and only Christmas card I'll ever get from an NBA player,' says one team official."[54]

Likewise, the Rockets wanted to make Yao feel at home. How could they do any less for the man featured on the cover of their Little Red Handbook (otherwise known as the team's media guide)? Rockets General Manager Carroll Dawson spoke on behalf of the entire organization: "Everybody loves him. He gets attention obviously, for the way he plays, but people also really like him and his personality. Everyone is curious, and they're finding out about him— more and more, when I go out, people will come up to me and say, 'I am not even a basketball fan, but I like watching Yao Ming.' The league has not had a kind of player like that in a long time."[55]

For his part, Yao increasingly enjoyed the camaraderie on the Rockets: "I feel I'm getting comfortable with the other teammates, we have been working hard in practice.... Everyone has been pretty fun to hang around. Boki [fellow rookie Bostjan Nachbar, the fifteenth pick in the 2002 draft] and I have hung out and we get along pretty well, but everyone is so young so it's fun to be around people the same age."[56]

Overall he appreciated the red carpet that the state and city rolled out for him: "What has really touched me is that they haven't just looked at me as a basketball player. They've treated me like a Texan and really taken me into their hearts." Early on, Yao got the royal treatment from politicos left and right. On October 24, 2002, he met former president George Bush and Chinese President Jiang Zemin. After taking a limousine ride to Bush's Presidential Library at Texas A&M, Yao was welcomed by George Sr. as "the newest Texan from China." Then Jiang, referring to Yao as "a national treasure," asked Yao to stand up.[57] After witnessing the raucous reception given Yao, Bush needled Jiang, "You're the second most recognizable Chinese face in America now."[58]

Not to be outdone, Houston's Mayor Lee Brown and the Chinese Consul General Hu Yeshun hosted a reception at the convention center to officially welcome Yao to their fair city. There Mayor Brown presented him a proclamation declaring December 11th "Yao Ming Day." Soon even Yao became a local booster, testifying, "The city has given me a very warm feeling. Whenever anybody greets me, they treat me like I'm a Texan, a new Texan. I've been in Dallas before ... and my impression was, 'It's really hot in the summer, the steak is really good, the area is very large, and the cities aren't that crowded.'"[59]

Yao isn't the only one to have felt that way. Texas was a magnet for migrants even before it was part of the US. Once liberated from Spain, Mexico intentionally attracted Americans to the territory in the 1820s, only to discover that the Anglo settlers refused to be assimilated into Mexican culture. As hostilities broke out, General Sam Houston spearheaded Texas' fight for independence from Mexico. For over a month, Houston played a frustrating game of "cat and mouse," avoiding a direct confrontation with Santa Anna's

THE TAO OF YAO

larger Imperial army. Then, crying "Remember the Alamo," Houston's band of 750 irregulars ambushed and routed 1,500 Mexican soldiers in the twenty-minute Battle of San Jacinto. A year later in 1837, as the Republic's first president, Houston authorized the incorporation of the city that would bear his name and become the first capital of the 28th state of the Union.

Now Houston covers more than 617 square miles and is the fourth largest city in the US, home to more than two million people. Almost 250,000 of them are Asian Americans, double the total of a decade ago, and a percentage twice that of the Texas average.[60] According to Rice University's *Houston Area Survey*, "Virtually all of the population growth that Harris County [of which Houston is a part] has experienced in the past fifteen years is due to the arrival of foreign immigrants, primarily from Asia and Latin America."[61] Logically Yao considered Houston's large Chinese community an asset to him, saying, "I think it will definitely help me adapt to the NBA. At least there will be a lot of Chinese restaurants around to help me adapt to the food easier."[62]

Last but not least, a key factor in Yao's speedy acclimation was his trusty interpreter Colin Pine. Hired as a desk jockey at the State Department, Pine was translating documents on the computer when he heard about the job opening. Beating out nearly four hundred applicants for the position, Pine left the office behind and was soon jet-setting around the country seated next to Shanghai's closest thing to a rock star. The bespectacled 28-year-old remembered that his 22-year-old boss' first impression of him was "I thought you would be older."[63]

© Oliver Chin

↞ Speak softly and carry a small translator.

"His life is his life and my life is my life and they are intertwined right now and I'm absolutely fine with that. He makes it so easy because he is such an easygoing, gentle person."[64]

—Colin Pine

THE TAO OF YAO

Knowing more English than he let on, Yao still relied on his translator to make life easier. It seemed whenever a question came Yao's way, Pine was there to help answer it. Soon their habit of speaking in tongues and in turns became so automatic that Yao said of his 5'10" blond-haired assistant, "When the sun comes out, so does my shadow."[65] As the pair became practically inseparable, Coach Rudy Tomjanovich accepted Yao's helper as just another member of the entourage: "There seems to be a bond that they've developed already. It's funny, though, because when I'm talking in the meetings, it's like, hey, there's an echo back there. Is that me?"[66]

So talented for putting words in Yao's mouth, Pine himself became a handy target for Yao's barbs. Selflessly Pine translated jokes at his own expense, as when Yao mock-threatened him, "I still don't understand a lot of things. If I did you would have been fired a while ago."[67]

But deep down Yao did appreciate the man who reliably mediated the world's full-court press. When asked what he was most grateful for before his first Thanksgiving, Yao replied, "Colin," and patted his companion on the back.[68] When asked how much he thought Americans understand about Chinese, Yao answered, "Not as much as my translator."[69] Then as his first season drew to a close, Yao complimented his erstwhile mouthpiece: "Colin has been a big help to me. I'll definitely recommend him to the next Chinese player in the NBA."[70]

Perhaps Yao was also thankful that he had a dependable buddy who was as much a novice to the NBA game of traveling and talking as he was. Trading places, Yao would have had fun interpreting his translator's faux pas when Pine's ringing cellphone interrupted a packed news conference. Speaking for himself this time, Pine apologized, "I am so sorry. I'm a rookie."[71]

With his first year almost under his belt, Yao had definitely come a long way. As proof of his successful acclimation, Yao finally got the seal of approval that he had long desired. In March 2003, he received his driver's license. After being coached by his mother, who already passed the driving test, Yao could finally fly solo. For a moment, he was no different from any other irrepressible youth who had his whole life ahead of him. Yao joked, "I really want to get the James Bond 007 BMW that has all the special features."[72]

Now Bill Walton considered Houston to be his new favorite destination. What was his reason? "Yao Ming. Nothing more need be said. . . . Is there anything Yao Ming can't do? We all have so much to learn from him. Why does everybody think it's the other way around? . . . Not many shopping days left for Yao Ming season tickets. And then there were none left and all were sad."[73]

Chapter 7

The Aim of Athletics

In his first NBA preseason game, Yao scored 6 points against the San Antonio Spurs. A month later, he scored 27 points and had 18 rebounds against them. "The biggest difference between the first game and this game, is that my confidence is much, much higher," he said.[1]

> *The truly wise are content to be last. They are, therefore, first.*
> *They are indifferent to themselves. They are, therefore, self-*
> *confident.*[2]
>
> —Lao Tzu

The late TV sportscaster Dick Schaap once commented, "If Lao-tzu, who wrote the original *Tao*, had seen DiMaggio and Griffey, Wilt and Michael, Jim Brown and Joe Montana, he might have been moved to compose a sports version of his classic."[3]

This insight is all too true. Today sports is one of the most absorbing and debated of all human activities. But like other pursuits, sports can be viewed as an incarnation of Taoism. For those who wonder how, writer Stephen Mitchell connects the dots:

[S]ports provides many of us with our first and strongest conscious experience of being 'in the Tao' or 'in the zone,' in the current of energy where the right action happens by itself, effortlessly.... It may seem odd at first to think of sports as a paradigm for life.... And it may be easier to learn the essential wisdom life has to teach us by paying closer attention to an activity that we passionately love. Wisdom is already there, in the perfect drop shot, in the blown lay-up; all we have to do is take the time to notice it. If only the lessons of life were as clear as the lessons of sports. But they are![4]

In an illustrious career that spanned from winning the basketball gold medal in the 1956 Melbourne Olympics to becoming one of the NBA's Top 50 players ever, Bill Russell relished these unpredictable, intoxicating, and fleeting moments of pure bliss:

The game would move so quickly that every fake, cut and pass would be surprising, and yet nothing could surprise me. It was almost as if we were playing in slow motion. During those spells I could almost sense how the next play would develop and where the next shot would be taken. Even before the other team brought the

---

"Developing the muscles of the soul demands no competitive spirit, no killer instinct, although it may erect pain barriers that the spiritual athlete must crash through."[5]

—Germaine Greer

ball in bounds, I could feel it so keenly that I'd want to shout to my teammates, 'It's coming there!'—except that I knew everything would change if I did. My premonitions would be consistently correct, and I always felt then that I not only knew all the Celtics by heart but also all the opposing players, and that they all knew me. There have been many times in my career when I felt moved or joyful, but these were the moments when I had chills pulsing up and down my spine.[6]

As an ancient form of sport, martial arts provide timeless lessons in how the body and the mind can be trained to become one. Called "master," the instructor commands the supreme respect of his pupils, who learn that the foundation of success lies in cultivating discipline over their mental and physical impulses. By focusing the mind, one can make the body's response a habit, automatic and unconscious. "The Wizard of Westwood," John Wooden, maintained that the same is true in basketball: "The proper execution of fundamentals can become instinctive if taught properly, just like breathing or walking."[7]

However, the game has changed. Today in the professional arena, sport is not seen as an end unto itself, but as a means to fame and fortune.

Contrary to popular belief, the Olympics are more of a recent construct than an ancient ideal. In 1896 the French aristocrat, fundraiser, and self-described "pedagogue" Pierre de Coubertin "revived" the mythic games to promote his idea of muscular diplomacy: "Let us export our oarsmen, our runners, our fencers into other lands. That is the true Free

Trade of the future; and the day it is introduced into Europe the cause of Peace will have received a new and strong ally."[8] But since then, the glorification of the amateur hobbyist has given way to the professional paid endorser. Despite the inspirational films of Bud Greenspan, the image of the five rings has become badly tarnished due to the bribery scandals and institutionalized corruption of the US and International Olympic Committees.

Nowadays, sportsmanship is known for what it isn't. We know the penalties by name, not the principles. Unnecessary roughness. Unsportsmanlike conduct. Flagrant fouls. In the age of television, the spoilsports are the ones who routinely draw the camera's eye.

Every sport has its poster child. In tennis it was John McEnroe in the 1980s: the London tabloids dubbed him "Super Brat" after he threw temper tantrums on Wimbledon's Centre Court. In baseball, Ty Cobb intentionally sharpened his spikes to terrorize second basemen with his slides, and his spiritual twin Pete Rose was banned for gambling on games. In the 2002 regular season, New York Yankees pitcher Roger Clemons beaned New York Mets catcher Mike Piazza. Later in a World Series confrontation, Clemons broke Piazza's bat with a pitch and flung a jagged piece of wood back at the batter in a spontaneous fit of rage. In football, New York Jets defensive end Mark Gastineau reveled in the sack dance over fallen quarterbacks. Then touchdown celebrations hit a new low when in 2002 San Francisco 49ers' wide receiver Terrell Owens crossed the goal line, signed the pigskin with a pen hidden in his sock, and handed it to his financial advisor in the end-zone.

But when the home team incessantly blares rock music and gives fans balloons to wave, signs to sway, and sticks to strike just to distract the visiting team, it is no surprise that sportsmanship can't be upheld on the field. Certainly buying a ticket gives one the right to jeer. But some would argue that the crowd mentality of "what have you done for me lately" has existed since the Romans egged on gladiators in the Coliseum. In the midst of it all, Bill Russell found the fans' treatment of him so paradoxically disturbing that he foreswore signing autographs altogether. "I've stood in the Boston Garden after making a big play in a play-off game and literally felt fifteen thousand people cheering for me—the whole Garden shaking with waves of emotion washing over me so strongly that it felt as if my spinal column were immersed in sparkling champagne," he writes. "And I have felt the personal abuse of those same fans—sometimes right after the game."[9]

He who knows does not speak.
He who speaks does not know.[10]

—Lao Tzu

Players too have pumped up the volume. Trash-talking is a mandatory survival skill in the NBA, where verbal sparring can be more bruising than the physical contact. Not knowing the language could help Yao block out the distractions, but it also made him an easy mark for taunts he otherwise wouldn't have tolerated. Yao was aware of this universal tactic even before he played his first NBA game.

THE TAO OF YAO

He said, "I'll teach every Rockets player Chinese trash-talking. We had foreign players on our [Shanghai] team. They learned to trash-talk before they learned any other Chinese."[11]

But defending bragging rights and turf is no laughing matter. Often players establish the pecking order on the floor to show who's the boss in the box score. "The better you are, the tougher it is. No. 1, when they find out you're really good, they start knocking you around. They start knocking you down and coming after you," stressed Bill Walton. "You have to learn how to protect yourself, because this isn't about milk and cookies. This is men playing nasty basketball at the highest level for the biggest prize."[12] Or as Charles Barkley once said, "When you're the top dog, everybody wants to put you in the pound."

The Detroit Pistons' Ben Wallace should know. This 6'9", 240-lb enforcer was the NBA's defensive player of the year for two straight years (2002–03), and in 2002 became only the fourth player ever to lead the NBA in both rebounds and blocked shots (joining Abdul-Jabbar, Walton, and Olajuwon). Back in the summer 2002 World Basketball Championships, Wallace relished the prospects of intimidating Yao:

> We are going to beat him up pretty bad. This is our way of saying, "This is our playground and this is how we play. Welcome to our country." We know around the NBA what hype is all about. People are just trying to sell tickets on the back of him, and it's going to be a good challenge for the big guy. Everybody in the league is going to step up and make him work for everything he gets. Nothing comes free in American basketball.[13]

So open season was declared on Yao. After being assaulted by the opposition early on in the year, Yao returned to the bench and complained, "That is not an honorable team."[14] It wasn't going to get easier, as Yao predicted that his adversaries would up the ante. "I think it will be tougher the second time around. I'm finding that it's getting more and more physical."[15]

March 31, 2003, was no different. That night New Jersey center Dikembe Mutombo elbowed Yao in the throat to help the Nets douse the Rockets 110–86. Renowned for his lethally sharp forearms, the 7'2" and 265-lb Mutombo excused the low blow by saying, "I can't believe my elbow can reach his neck. I thought I was going to get it between his chest and stomach and box him out. Next thing I knew he was on the floor. I didn't realize that so I told him to 'get up.'" Ending with 24 points, Yao was obviously derailed after crashing to the court clutching his windpipe in the second quarter. But again taking the high road, Yao gave Mutombo a backhanded compliment: "I think his face is a little bit cuter than his elbow."[16]

> *Those who are skilled as soldiers don't seem warlike,*
> *those skilled at fighting don't seem angry,*
> *those skilled in defeating the foe don't engage them,*
> *those skilled at employing others*
> *deem themselves inferior.*[17]
>
> —Lao Tzu

Houston's coach Rudy Tomjanovich marveled at how Yao managed to maintain his cool while being on the

> "Being the first overall pick in the NBA draft doesn't necessarily guarantee individual stardom or even immediate team success. But [the 2002] top pick, Houston's Yao Ming, is having the kind of impact in his first season that could earmark the Rockets as a team of the future."[18]
>
> —*USA Today*

receiving end of the NBA's notoriously rough play: "Yao just accepts it as a part of the game. He may get mad at himself, but I've seen situations where veteran guys get physical, and all of a sudden, they're blowing a gasket. He has a very even temperament."[19] The coach knows what it's like to be on both ends when tempers flare. Remembering a fight he had in his second season (and his first in Houston), Tomjanovich acknowledged, "It was amazing to me how quickly you kind of lose control in a situation like that. Your adrenaline gets going and you are doing things you know you shouldn't do. When it was over, I felt ashamed of myself for losing it that way. That memory stayed with me quite clearly. I didn't want it to happen again."[20]

Keeping level-headed is one thing. But being a role model is another. This notion has become literally a foreign concept in an era subject to free agency, salary caps, labor strikes, lockouts, owner collusion, and drug abuse. Sports fans have wondered whether chivalry is really dead, gone the way of philanthropists such as Pittsburgh Pirate outfielder Roberto Clemente (who in 1972 died in a plane crash while delivering earthquake relief supplies in Nicaragua) or classy and tactful pioneers such as tennis' Arthur Ashe (campaigning for treatment against AIDS, a disease that eventually would take his life). Nonetheless, a code of honor survives, as some athletes carry themselves well both off the court and on it, and can be as humble in winning as they are gracious in defeat. Yao said, "There's nothing I can really say [to please the critics]. Basketball is not something that you can talk about, it's an action through which you can show people. I just think I need to show them on the court."[21]

From the very beginning of his NBA career, Yao was quick to criticize himself. After a loss in which he was held scoreless, Yao refused to sugarcoat his play: "I was a little bit sorry for my performance. But that's the reality I have to face."[22] After the Rockets were defeated by the New York Knicks, Yao concluded, "I think at the end of the game, if it wasn't for my turnovers, the game would have been different."[23] Yet after losing to the Dallas Mavericks, Yao pointed out that all was not really lost: "You have to understand that I look at the game in two parts—one part is the enjoyment of playing, the other part is winning. Today, I achieved half of that."[24]

These words resonated with those from wise predecessors. Only two men have been enshrined in the Hall of Fame as both a player and a coach. The first was John Wooden. His protégé Kareem Abdul-Jabbar recalled Wooden preaching, "We may not win, but let's make it worthy of us."[25] The second was Lenny Wilkens, who is the NBA's all-time winningest coach. Before resigning as coach of the Toronto Raptors later in the 2002–03 campaign, Wilkens evaluated Yao: "I think he's gotten better as the season has gone on.

He's much more comfortable. And they've learned to play with him a whole lot better. And that's what it takes. He's made tremendous strides. And he's going to be a terrific player."[26]

Jeff Van Gundy, whose father Bill Van Gundy coached for four decades and whose brother Stan is an assistant coach for Pat Riley's Miami Heat, also applauded Yao, saying, "The guy is what our league, as far as people, should be about. Everyone in the game from youth teams on up can learn a lot from the way he approaches the game with both enthusiasm and humility. He's a very good player who's come in with more hype than any rookie in a long, long time. And he's lived up to it and surpassed it because of his unbelievable demeanor."[27] In the grand scheme of things, Van Gundy said, "People fail for different reasons, but the rare combination is talent and character. Yao, just watching him, is one of those who has got both."[28]

Therefore nobility is rooted in humility,
loftiness is based on lowliness.[29]

—Lao Tzu

Sensing the winds of change, *ESPN The Magazine* remarked that Yao's refreshing attitude "blows through the NBA like a blast of fresh air into a collapsed mine shaft."[30] Yet again Bill Walton was impressed: "It's amazing Yao has been able to stay so upbeat, smiling and friendly. There's none of the anger and bitterness and defensiveness that virtually every player in our society and culture grows up with. Fans see him as a real hope and dream that there is something really good out there. We need those positive images and role models."[31]

For his part Yao was straightforward in what he hoped to accomplish. "I hope through me, people will be more interested in basketball," he said. "This is a great sport to get into, to play and participate in. And this is what I want other people to remember, through me, to understand through me."[32]

With this statement, Yao inserted himself into a long-standing Asian tradition of respecting one's elders and fore-fathers. When his Shanghai Sharks team won the Chinese Basketball Association championship in April 2002 (Yao scored 44 points and snared 21 rebounds in the clincher), Yao obediently professed that his predecessors deserved the credit, not him. "At the time, I thought about all the players that had come before me in Shanghai, who had the same goal for us, who had worked very hard for it, and we were only the lucky ones who were able to reap the fruit of their work."[33]

On January 6, 2003, Yao became the first athlete in Chinese sports history to have his jersey retired. In the face of such acclaim, Yao could only cite his regrets about being singled out: "There are a lot of athletes in the history of China that are qualified to have their numbers retired as well. So I feel fortunate to be the first. . . . My father also wore the No. 15 when he played. I guess the only thing I feel sorry about is that my son might not be able to wear the number."[34] Watching his oversize Shanghai Sharks #15 jersey (woven ten times the actual size) raised into Luwan

Stadium's rafters, Yao was touched. "It is really significant to me. I am very grateful to all the fans for their support."[35] Yao meant what he said. Purchasing a full-page ad in Shanghai's biggest newspaper, he properly used the following Chinese adage as its headline: "How does a single blade of grass thank the sun?"[36]

There Is No "I" in Team

A leader is best when people barely know he exists; when his work is done, his aim fulfilled, they will say: we did it ourselves.[37]
—Lao Tzu

Chinese basketball culture is a lot like international basketball, like FIBA basketball. You have to understand that I feel I am a part of the team. If the team loses, I am responsible for that. I only feel I have done my job if the team wins. My only goal is to help the team win if I can do it.[38]
—Yao Ming

The Chicago Bears running back Gayle Sayers, in his famous story of his friendship with teammate Brian Piccolo, wrote, "God is first, friends and family are second, and I am third." Yao shared a similar belief: "I think I'll stick to what I'm used to, my principle, and that is team No. 1 and individual No. 2. I remember going to an NBA training facility, and I remember seeing a very large letter on the wall, saying 'no one's bigger than the team.'"[39]

But first he had to be accepted by the team and its captain. Steve Francis was nicknamed "The Franchise" for a reason.

The point guard's first season of 1999–2000 had surpassed all expectations. He was co-Rookie of the Year, the first Rocket ever to get 400 rebounds and give 500 assists in one season, and was the first Houston rookie to lead the team in points, assists, and steals. With over 18 points a game in his first year, he increased his scoring average every year thereafter, following in the footsteps of the legendary Elgin Baylor. On track to earning his second straight All-Star berth in 2002–03, Francis was the best player on a team that had nowhere to go but up.

Then along came Yao. Some wondered how the former Maryland Terrapin would react. But Francis put those fears to rest by embracing his new teammate, just as Charles Barkley once had with him. Naming the newcomer "Dynasty," Francis announced, "That is even bigger than 'Franchise,'" and then ordered custom "Ming Dynasty" pants made for Yao. Asked why he took Yao so quickly under his wing, Francis said, "Basketball is universal. As a player, you respect talent no matter what."[40] Though Yao was born half a world away, Francis found him to be on the same wavelength: "He'll know when guys are upset, and he asks if they're OK. He speaks another language to you guys, but he doesn't speak another language in the locker room."[41]

"I just told him to be patient, just like Hakeem told me. It's funny. You really learn that the cycle of players continues. The NBA was here before me, and it'll be here after me—at first, you couldn't have told me that. No way."[42]

—Steve Francis

Yao was typically deferential, commenting, "It's important for us to be good friends, but I don't think I'm qualified to be a leader on this team. I'm only a rookie."[43]

Even before the season started, Francis said, "I know he's younger than me, but I think he's my big brother already."[44] Then the 6'3", 200-lb guard characterized his relationship with his new pal: "He's just like me, only 7-5 and Chinese."[45] The future looked so bright, Francis was tempted to wear shades. "It's good to see for years to come, we're going to be Batman and Robin. Who's Batman and who's Robin, I don't know. We're going to be like that from now on. It's going to be great."[46]

When informed that Francis had vowed to make Yao the league's MVP, the center smirked, "I'm so touched I feel like crying."[47]

However, they weren't Houston's first odd couple. Rudy Tomjanovich and Calvin Murphy were. Both were drafted in 1970 while the team was still based in San Diego. An All-American from the University of Michigan, Tomjanovich was the #2 pick. At Niagara College, Murphy owned the fourth-highest scoring average in NCAA history, and was picked #18 in the second round. As rookies, the two started bunking together on the road, and they would remain roommates long after players could get their own individual accommodations. As Murphy told sportswriter John Feinstein, "I never had a brother. Until Rudy."[48] Known for his fearlessness, this 5'10" sparkplug tirelessly combated the stigma of being the "little guy" and ultimately was rewarded. His #23 followed Tomjanovich's into retirement in 1984, and "The Greatest Rocket of Them All" dashed into the Hall of Fame in 1993. Now a TV commentator for the team, he said of his friend, "He was about the only guy who could say to me, 'Calvin, you're wrong,' and I would listen."[49]

Twenty years later, Houston was glad to have another dynamic duo. The MVP of the 2002 World Basketball Championships, Germany's Dirk Nowitzki, marveled, "It's amazing how [Yao] gets in his first year and is able to adjust to everything and already has an impact on his team."[50] The Rockets thought so too. Forward Glen Rice gave a sigh of relief. Previously Shaq's teammate on the Lakers' 1999–2000 championship team, Rice valued what a big man could do. "Yao Ming, I tell you what, thank God he is on our team," Rice noted. "This guy has a tremendous amount of skill, both offensively and defensively."[51] Guard Cuttino Mobley added, "I love him. You only have to tell him stuff one time and he listens. He's not a cocky kid. He's lovable. I just love playing with him. It takes a lot of pressure off myself. I don't have to go as crazy out there. It's great to have somebody that big down low that has that much of an impact."[52]

Even when sitting on the bench, athletes can be positive influences. Though preferring to play, Yao knew better than to sulk when he didn't. "It didn't feel good and I want to contribute but I have to offer encouragement when I'm not playing."[53] Learning through observation instead of action, Yao realized that a true teammate provides moral support with the right frame of mind.

Chemistry is an intangible. It isn't something you can draft, trade for, or buy. But camaraderie is an essential ingredient to a team's success. Not wanting to upset the balance, Yao wished to blend in, prove his dependability, and fortify his team's collective skills. After a loss, Yao said, "I think we just need to improve our chemistry, work on passing the ball around and having more faith in our teammates. We need to get stronger mentally. We don't have the experience yet, basketball experience and competitive experience."[54]

Yao had entered the NBA at a time when coaches lamented the demise of players' skills and attitudes. More kids than ever are bypassing college to go pro in hopes of cashing in. Thrust into the big pond to sink or swim, it's "everyone for themselves" as players pursue individual success first, and team success second. Only at the end of their careers do veteran free-agents gladly accept reduced roles and salary for the shot at winning a ring. Cases in point are 35-year-old Gary "The Glove" Payton and 40-year-old Karl "The Mailman" Malone. This duo sent shockwaves through the NBA by signing with the Los Angeles Lakers (recently thwarted in their bid for a fourth-straight title by the San Antonio Spurs) for the 2003–04 season. Nine-time All-Star and first-team All-Defense, point guard Payton settled for $8 million less per year than what he earned with the Milwaukee Bucks. Second to Kareem Abdul-Jabbar as the all-time NBA scoring leader, Malone was an eight-time All-Star and two-time league MVP with the Utah Jazz. The power forward went even further and took a 90% pay cut (almost $18 million) for the chance to finally taste the champion's champagne.

A noted disciplinarian, 6'10" John Thompson was Bill Russell's back-up on the Boston Celtics, and, formerly the coach of Georgetown Hoyas, he shepherded Patrick Ewing, Alonzo Mourning, Dikembe Mutombo, and Allen Iverson to NBA stardom. Now a basketball commentator, Thompson noted that the decline of young players' skills coincided with the increase in foreign players in the NBA:

> A lot of this is the result of the complacency and laziness of American players. Some kids work hard and do what they are supposed to do, but a lot of them have sugar plums in their head about making a lot of money and going to the NBA. We've created a system where rather than being told what to do, the player is telling people what he wants. The high school guy, the AAU guy and the college guy are all kissing his butt, and the kid gets full of himself and how good you think he is, instead of doing the work to get there.[55]

Rob Bobcock, the Minnesota Timberwolves' director of player personnel, concurred: "What we're drafting today are basketball athletes, not basketball players. Very few of them have acquired much skill. These guys just don't know how to play. We need to get back to teaching the values of the game. Our kids have the attitude that they're going to dunk on you every time down the court. Sometimes, it's as if whoever has the ball when it crosses halfcourt is pretty much going to take the shot. We're seeing too many poor shooters, too many rushed shots, and until we make the effort to teach, the international players will have the advantage."[56]

Byron Scott could identify with this from his personal experience. The beneficiary of Magic Johnson's largesse as his backcourt mate on the Lakers, Scott won three NBA championships and became the team's all-time career leader in three-point field goals made. He concluded his career overseas, signing the largest contract in European basketball history, helping the Athenian team Panathinaikos win its first Greek Professional League title in thirteen years, and becoming a 1997–98 European All-Star and Most Valuable Player. Emulating his mentor Pat Riley, Scott began his coaching career by assisting Rick Adelman with the Sacramento Kings. Then in 2000 he took the reins of the New Jersey Nets and led them to two straight NBA finals. Scott reckoned, "I think the [2002] draft definitely sent a message. All our kids want to do is dunk and run. They've got to get back to fundamentals. The guys over there work a lot harder on shooting and dribbling and passing, and in a lot of cases they are doing more with less talent."[57]

Recognized as one of the best passing centers today, Vlade Divac tossed in, "I watch some high school games here and in L.A., and I see these big, strong kids, and all they do is dunk. Nobody teaches them the fundamentals. But in Europe and overseas, they still teach those things. So it is good to see a 7-footer with those skills come into the league. There aren't too many of us left."[58]

The Forgotten Fundamentals

Not to value one's teacher,
not to value one's material;
though this seems clever,
it is actually great delusion—
this is the essential secret.[59]

—Lao Tzu

Yao recalls the gauntlet of exercises he had to complete when he was fourteen: "We had to be at the court at six o'clock in the morning. We wouldn't eat breakfast first. We'd go distance running. After running, you would have to make 100 shots. Then you would eat breakfast and rest for a little while. Half an hour later you would resume practicing." Training was his job, and at least three days a week Yao endured ten hours of practice that were broken into four sessions. On the weekends he couldn't bear facing the thought of Monday's drills. At the memory Yao grimaced, "I was always a little sad. At that time, I guess I really didn't have a choice. If I had to do it again, I don't think I could do it."[60]

John Wooden led UCLA to a record ten NCAA basketball titles, including an unparalleled seven straight from 1966 to 1973. The hallmark of his teams was the emphasis on individual fundamentals as the key ingredient for a team's success. Wooden said, "There is no replacement for sound fundamentals and strict discipline. They will reinforce you in the toughest circumstance."[61] One of his most beloved pupils, Kareem recalled:

All of our practices revolved around the running game and the three pieces of Coach Wooden's system: conditioning, fundamentals, and teamwork. After college, I never again experienced practices like his. Every drill had a precise purpose and was precisely timed. You would advance from one drill to the next and to the next, without stopping or doubling back to repeat a drill. Every workout was a tightly structured grid laid over the anticipated rising fatigue of the players. Every day had its own practice plan, but you knew to expect an exactitude and the practice would end on time, a certainty that eased the toughness of the hour and forty-five minutes, which was usually how long we would go. Everybody did everything. The guards took the big-man drills and the big men worked at the guards' drills. It was my first serious training program and, as it turned out, the best training for the pros I could have had.[62]

Kareem's successor Bill Walton felt identically. Growing up in San Diego, Walton was such an outstanding high school prospect that his coach gave him the keys to the gym. Then Walton would open it up for the waiting players from the Rockets such as Pat Riley and Rick Adelman so they could run all night.[63] But Walton got his true basketball education once he went to college:

> One of the greatest things that Coach Wooden taught us—and he taught us so much—was how to learn. The learning process is an acquired skill. On my very first day as a freshman player at UCLA, Coach Wooden walked into the locker room, pulled up a stool, sat down and told us exactly how he wanted us to put on our socks, how to lace our shoes, how to put on those shoes, how to tuck our jerseys in, how to tie the drawstrings in our pants, how to dry our hair after practice. He showed us how to warm up, how to shoot a jump shot, how to eat properly, how to organize our day, how and when to sleep. No detail was too small.... But instead of giving

THE TAO OF YAO

us the ball and pointing us toward the court, Coach Wooden knew it was more important to first teach the most basic of skills. A solid, indestructible foundation. . . . The purpose of all this was to show us the importance of starting with the basics, of mastering those basics and then moving on to the next level. After all, once you learn how to teach yourself something, you can do anything.[64]

In the same way Yao's work ethic was instilled early on. Yao remembered trying out for the Shanghai Sharks junior team. "Endurance, strength, it's like what you would see in a sports movie, doing all these drills. And we did some things maybe you don't know about. Some strange things that help improve your reaction time, the strength and feel of your fingers and wrists." These were not necessarily fond memories for Yao since "everybody complained. It was extremely tiring. . . . That kind of training doesn't exist anymore. I was unlucky. I was in the last group to do that."[65]

Regarded by many as the most influential basketball coach ever, Pete Newell left fingerprints all over the modern game. He was the first coach to win the NIT, NCAA, and Olympic basketball titles (University of San Francisco's 1949 NIT title, UC Berkeley's 1959 NCAA title, and he led Jerry West and Oscar Robertson to gold in the 1960 Rome Olympics). Also Newell was the bane of John Wooden as his Bears defeated the UCLA Bruins in his last eight meetings (1957–60). Interviewed by sportswriter

© Merv Lopes

"You are going to see the amount of international players continue to increase because they are coming into the NBA more skillful than the players who've been in the league for three or four years. Just look at Yao Ming."[66]

—Pete Newell

THE TAO OF YAO

Bruce Jenkins, former University of Indiana coach Bobby Knight expressed his profound respect for Newell's acumen:

> When you really examine it, you realize how far ahead Pete is over everyone else. He's had a longer involvement with the teaching of the game than anyone in history.... Most outstanding coaches have particular strengths, but Pete is the only one I know who is strong in every facet of the game. There isn't any aspect of it, from balance and footwork to attacking the most intricate of defenses, that Pete can't teach. Think of all the significant rule changes he's witnessed: the elimination of the center jump, the 10-second violation, the widening of the free-throw lane, the three-point shot and the shot clock, along with the myriad of different points of emphasis from an officiating standpoint. Who's the one person, over all that time, who has been constant with his involvement in the game? Newell. His influence is so great, going back so many years, a lot of coaches are completely unaware that the concepts they're using can be traced back to Pete and his coaching strategies at USF, Michigan State and California. I don't think that anyone has studied the history of basketball any more than I have, and I put Pete at the top of the list. He's simply the best there ever was.[67]

Newell's calling card was his obsession with fundamentals. A case in point was the genesis of Newell's celebrated "Big Man Camp": Newell decided to help turn around the floundering career of Kermit Washington, who had been the Los Angeles Lakers' first-round pick (#5 overall) in 1973 when Newell was General Manager. After Washington awkwardly fouled him during a game, Golden State's Rick Barry chastised him, "Listen, you better learn how to play this game." So in the summer of 1976 Washington surrendered his fate to the hands of an old master. David Halberstam wrote, "The first few weeks were terrible ... in the privacy of the gym, [Newell] was radically different, tough, demanding, the coach as drill sergeant.... The drills were relentless, three hours of them, repeated and repeated until Washington did not know which was more ready to collapse, his brain or his body. Each day when he came home he was unable to walk for two or three hours."[68]

As rumor spread of the training's benefits, Newell's groups ironically got bigger. A former thirteen-year NBA veteran, Kiki Vandeweghe had played at UCLA under coach Larry Brown. As an undergraduate, he was one of the first ones to join Newell's "camp," and later became a loyal instructor. Now General Manager of the Denver Nuggets, Vandeweghe says his experience was "Like the Bataan death march. I remember Kermit just beating on me every single day. But it was the best thing that ever happened to me."[69] In Newell's biography *A Good Man*, Washington winced that once Vandeweghe joined, "Now we had even harder drills. It was like a living nightmare every day. Drills over and over again. You wanted to faint, but you knew if you did, and a fire started, you wouldn't feel like getting up. You'd just burn there. It would be easier to die."[70]

But comparing the "before" and "after" Washington, Lakers coach Jerry West was floored. "He was a different player,

> "Yao is the next step up the evolutionary ladder of big men in a game in which our perception of what is possible is always being tested, in which they long ago stopped pushing the envelope and broke right through it."[71]
>
> —*Houston Chronicle*

especially on offense, but on defense too. I had thought of him before as someone you couldn't play for long stretches, because it was like playing four-on-five on offense and you couldn't do that. But he had moves now, he could make something happen facing the basket. He had made himself into a power forward."[72]

Two decades later, now Newell turned his keen eye to appraise the newcomer from China. "[Yao] epitomizes what other countries are doing and we are not: They're really teaching kids the fundamentals of the game," said Newell.[73] "Yao's a product of what [other countries] have been doing with players when they're 10 and 12 years old. They're teaching them the fundamentals, which we don't do any more. As a result he executes a lot of things in a fundamental way that really gets your attention, because he's only 21. His game seems to fit into the NBA game, and his lateral movement is unusually good for a fellow that size. He's such an athletic guy, and he's been taught a lot of foot skills in the paint area."[74]

Flip Saunders agreed. At the University of Minnesota he was a teammate of Kevin McHale, a future NBA Hall of Famer and Top 50 player ever, who won three titles with Larry Bird's Boston Celtics. Later he went on to coach in the

Continental Basketball Association, win two CBA championships (1990, 1992) and two Coach of the Year honors (1989, 1992). Then he rejoined McHale, who was General Manager of the Minnesota Timberwolves, to coach the sensational Kevin Garnett. "Yao Ming has great body balance. If he was 6-foot-8, he would be a guy who could play. The size is just an advantage," Saunders said. "The most impressive thing about Yao Ming is his fundamentals. He's so sound. He has extremely good footwork. His understanding of the game, where people should go, where he should screen people, what he should do if say [Steve] Francis is double-teamed is very, very astounding for a rookie."[75]

The Passing Principle

He who obtains has little. He who scatters has much.[76]
　　　　　　　—Lao Tzu

When I'm seeing them score points, it feels like I'm scoring points myself.[77]
　　　　　　　—Yao Ming

As General Manager of the San Diego Rockets in 1968 (before the team was sold and relocated to Houston), Newell was the man responsible for picking Rudy Tomjanovich and Calvin Murphy. Detractors roundly criticized him for both decisions, not knowing that they would become the two cornerstones of the franchise for decades to come. Defending his choice of Rudy over the aptly named Pistol Pete Maravich (graduating from Louisiana State University, Maravich was the leading scorer in NCAA history with an average of 44 points per game), Newell prioritized the intangibles of teamwork, saying, "When I looked at Rudy, I saw a guy who could do a lot of things: he could score, he could rebound, he could run the floor, and he could shoot the ball from deep at 6-8.... Basketball's a team game. I thought long-term Rudy was a better pick for us."[78]

Now Newell sized up Yao's potential as a blue-chip prospect and team player:

With him, the [added] height is certainly not a disadvantage—it's a tremendous advantage. Maybe I'm a little prejudiced on a player like this, because I'm pro-post players, but he's such a good passer. If you're 6-10, 6-11, 7 feet, you're eyeball-to-eyeball with your defender. When you're 7-6, you're many inches taller and you have a great visual scan. You're looking over people, not by them. And a player of that size doesn't have any worry of a guard double-teaming him, as long as he keeps [the ball] at chest level.[79]

A key skill that separated Yao from the average player was his willingness and ability to pass the basketball. After a win, Yao said, "I think passing is a very unique art. I enjoy it. I hope others do, too. I think it brings teammates together. Tonight we had many assists, and you can see what it did for us."[80]

After the US trounced China 84–54 in the summertime 2002 World Basketball Championships, the menacing Ben Wallace grudgingly gave Yao his due:

He's got a nice touch and a couple of post moves, a couple of good moves around the basket. To my surprise, he was a whole lot better than I thought he was. . . . I was surprised by his awareness on the court. When he caught the ball deep in the paint, he didn't waste time; he went into his move and made shots around the basket. When he caught it outside he turned and faced up and was able to find the open guy. That was impressive for a guy 7-5.[81]

Usually the province of the point guard, passing has become an undervalued art. Moreover, it is a rare skill among centers, who never get the ball as often as they'd like. But for those aware of the Tao, selfishness can easily become selflessness. After having a great scoring streak, Yao knew that he had become a bigger magnet for opponents' attention. But a patient center who dishes off well becomes even more dangerous. Effectively distributing the ball to his teammates provides the team better scoring opportunities. Said Yao, "My assists have increased because people are looking at me as an offensive threat. When I get the ball I have to pay attention to my teammates as well."[82]

Moses Malone liked what he saw: "Kid's got skills. Such great ability on top of all that 7-5 size. You can see he knows the game. . . . Yao is a great passer. He can read the game, understand what's going on."[83] ESPN's Bill Simmons wondered, "And when was the last time you saw a 7-footer start fastbreaks with 50-foot jai alai passes, or find open teammates with backdoor looks? In the Me-Me-Me NBA, that stuff isn't supposed to happen."[84] Winning the gold medal at the 2002 World Basketball Championships, the fundamentally sound Yugoslavians shocked Team USA, and made observers worldwide wonder if the American system has lost its edge. The Yugoslavian center, Vlade Divac, confirmed that Yao had what it took: "Every time I play him, he continued to play better and better. He's definitely going to be a great player in this league. I really like the way he thinks on the court, plays very unselfishly and understands the concept of the game."[85]

Yao considered the consequences of opponents' redoubled efforts to stop him: "I think it will definitely take away from my ability to some degree. Since people are already double-teaming me, it's something I am used to, and I like passing the ball."[86] Even after an evening of being stifled individually, Yao still highlighted the significance of moving the ball around. "It's not that I feel that I have to touch the ball all of the time," he said. "But I want to see more effective passes from all of our team. Tonight, I didn't think many of our passes were effective enough."[87]

"He's going to be a great player in this league," predicted Orlando's Tracy McGrady, considering Yao's attitude and talent. Going hardship in 1997 from Mt. Zion High School in Durham, North Carolina, the 6'8" small forward steadily climbed the NBA's ladder of success. The Most Improved Player in 2000–2001 and second team All-Star, he joined the All-NBA First Team in 2001–2002, and then became the league's leading scorer in 2003. T-Mac continued, "Once [Yao] gets some games under his belt and gets comfortable with the game, he's going to be unbelievable. And he just takes a lot out of you. He's so big and hard to double-team because he can just look over the double-team and pass out of that with ease. He rebounds. Guys do a great job playing off him when he passes the ball. He's a handful, man."[88]

But even Yao would want to stop passing the rock at some point and take a glamorous shot himself. After feeding and screening Francis for game-winning three-pointers, Yao noted, "Not only do I think we understand this play very well, but we've used it several times, I think other teams might as well. Maybe we should change it around, and next I should shoot the 3."[89] Eventually Yao's wish was granted. To seal a victory over Golden State later in the year, Francis penetrated to the hole and kicked the ball out to Yao, who was camped at the three-point line. Swish. Yao's first and only trifecta of the season brought peals of laughter from the Rockets' bench and a joyous bear hug from Francis.

Three-time ABA All-Star and three-time Coach of the Year, Larry Brown is the ninth-winningest coach in NBA history. Appreciating the value of discipline, as coach of the Philadelphia 76ers Brown had the formidable and draining task of corralling Allen Iverson, who was as volatile on the court as off it. Having his fill of players who have police records and require adult supervision, Brown said of Yao: "It's hysterical. A kid from China knows how to play and we've got kids in America who have no clue that are playing in our league."[90]

Rockets coach Rudy Tomjanovich recapped, "The guy is playing good. [For] a fan, he's enjoyable to watch. He does things the fundamental way on his passing and some of the things he does, and he's good for basketball—not only basketball here in the United States but basketball all over the world. It's what we've been saying all along [about Yao]. He's special. He has special vision, special poise, special skills."[91]

Indeed, Yao would need all these qualities to survive even bigger battles to come.

Chapter 8

Sports Are War

There is no disaster greater than thinking there is not an enemy—think that there is no enemy and you may almost lose your treasure.[1]

—Lao Tzu

If there is no conflict—internal or external—there can be no growth.[2]

—Sun Tzu

The best way to show your respect to your opponent is doing your best to beat him.[3]

—Yao Ming

Having led his teams to a record nineteen consecutive play-offs from 1982 to 2001, Pat Riley qualifies as one of the top ten NBA coaches of all time. But in 1984 when his Los

---

◀ "Baseball happens to be a game of cumulative tension but football, basketball, and hockey are played with hand grenades and machine guns."[4]

—John Leonard, *The New York Times*

Angeles Lakers lost the seventh game of the finals to the Celtics in the stifling Boston Garden, Riley was truly miserable. The Celtics' streak survived: they had met the Lakers for the title eight times, and they had never lost. Shellshocked by this demoralizing setback, Riley managed to find inspiration when he least expected it. "One afternoon in the following summer, as I was attending a coaching clinic by the University of Indiana coach Bobby Knight, he said, 'Anytime you have problems, this will give you a few things to think about,'" recollected Riley. "The book he recommended was *The Art of War*, written by Sun Tzu, a Chinese military commander who'd lived near the time of Confucius."[5] It was no coincidence that the very next season Riley got the leprechaun off his back by defeating the Celtics in the finals, and the Lakers repeated the feat in 1987.

So what does this ancient tome have to do with modern basketball?

For starters, Bill Russell wrote, "I think of all sports as a mixture of art and war."[6]

"Sports cut across racial, language, cultural, and national boundaries," proposed Hakeem Olajuwon in his autobiography. "It is what countries should use to compete instead of war."[7]

Recalling how seriously Jeff Van Gundy coached the New York Knicks, Patrick Ewing shivered, "When we lost, it was like we lost World War III."[8]

"A basketball team is like a band of warriors, a secret society with rites of initiation, a strict code of honor, and a sacred quest—the drive for the championship trophy," meditated nine-time NBA championship coach Phil Jackson in his book *Sacred Hoops*.[9]

THE TAO OF YAO

In his first NBA regular-season game against the Indiana Pacers, Yao confessed that he felt like a green recruit on the Western front. "In all aspects, it felt like a war. I did just so-so today. I was a little bit nervous and over-excited because I knew that millions of people were watching this game."[10]

Among other notable discoveries such as paper and printing, the Chinese invented gunpowder in the eighth century A.D. and used hollow bamboo stalks as rocket tubes, especially to launch festive pyrotechnics. Even with a few months of experience under his belt, Yao would describe a scoring spree like Francis Scott Key: "Watching everyone get their shots off like that was like watching fireworks all over the sky. It was coming from everywhere."[11]

If Sun Tzu had a ringside seat, undoubtedly he would have agreed. He wrote *The Art of War* during the fifth century B.C., right around when Taoism was founded. Though many assume Taoism is concerned purely with the pursuit of peace and tranquility, in fact, it reflects the time of turmoil in which it was born. In this chaotic era the Chinese countryside was wracked by internal dissension among feuding states. Gradually becoming a spiritual pillar of the culture at large, Taoism influenced the philosophy of not only health and medicine, and government and education, but also martial arts and military strategy. Thus war was seen as just another extension of daily life, and another arena where one's behavior should remain consistent with the Tao.

In Oliver Stone's movie *Wall Street*, the domineering tycoon Gordon Gekko (played by the actor Michael Douglas) is an infamous proponent for Sun Tzu. But as it turns out, the brash Gekko is a misleading role model. In actuality

Sun Tzu rejects the aggressive, bloodthirsty mentality of a corporate raider.

> *It must be understood that the most impressive victory is the one where no force is used.*[12]
>
> —Sun Tzu

Sun Tzu advocates a balanced state of mind, open to all possibilities, both offensive and defensive. The first art to master is gaining control over one's own thoughts, goals, and actions. In the film, Gekko cannot control his own belligerent impulses and is doomed by his excessive pride and greed. Sun Tzu would not have considered him a faithful disciple. If you cannot master your self, you have no business hoping that you can defeat anyone else.

Enemy Mine

> *Those who overcome others are powerful;*
> *those who overcome themselves are strong.*[13]
>
> —Lao Tzu

> *In ancient days warriors made themselves unbeatable by constant practice. Knowing they could never become invincible, their efforts enabled them to see the vulnerability of intended victims. They did not think in terms of beating the enemy by overwhelming him with boastful actions, but rather, they saw the reality of extending their skills through the enemy, which they acknowledged was the same thing as physical combat.*[14]
>
> —Sun Tzu

Of Sun Tzu's masterpiece Pat Riley said, "It's the earliest known study of warfare, and after twenty-five centuries, *The Art of War* still influences new generations. Napoleon used it. Mao Zedong used its advice to expel Chiang Kai-shek's larger, better supplied armies to the island of Taiwan. Afterward Mao wrote: 'We must not belittle the saying in the book of Sun Wu Tzu, the great military expert of ancient China, "Know your enemy and know yourself and you can fight a hundred battles without disaster."'"[15]

Yao was well acquainted with the martial mindset. In fact, one of his heroes is General Zhu Geliang, a prime minister of the Shu Kingdom (220–263 A.D.). In a well-known tale, an unreasonable army officer ordered Zhu to make 100,000 arrows in ten days. Zhu realized that manufacturing them was impossible, so he did the next best thing. On a foggy day he floated straw bales on the Yangtze River, pretending they were ships sailing for war to deceive his foe across the shore. In short order his "fleet" was covered in enemy arrows, and stealthily Zhu retrieved them all shortly thereafter. In admiration Yao said, "Ge didn't use power. He used his head."[16]

But in his first NBA practice, Yao was stunned by the rapid fire he encountered on the floor. "It's really fast. How quickly? I guess every time we [in China] were waiting for the shot clock to get to eight seconds. Here, maybe only 10 seconds or maybe 15 seconds to shoot. But I like it . . . a lot of shooting."[17]

Basketball terminology is rife with references to armed conflict: sharpshooters, gunners, and long-range bombs on the offense; traps, double teams, and collapsing zones on the defense. Still Yao knew he had to adjust to this run-and-gun style. "Before I was on the Chinese national team, and I was used to their strategy. The NBA is a different game, and I have to get used to it. I don't think I have been able to show the best of my abilities yet. I'm not quite used to the speed of the game, especially on offense."[18]

Drilled by basketball taskmaster Adolph Rupp at Kentucky, Pat Riley was the San Diego Rockets' first-round pick in their debut 1967–68 season. A teammate of Jerry West and Wilt Chamberlain's for the champion 1971–72 Lakers, the 6'4" forward wrapped up his career in 1976 with the Phoenix Suns. Informed by his thirty-plus years clashing in the NBA as both player and coach, Riley once solemnly intoned, "It isn't enough just to play the game—the Showtime Warrior wants to leave the mark of his will on the game itself."[19] Though this dictum sounds pretentious, it is true that the great athletes are driven by such overwhelming willpower that they will not take "no" for an answer. Moses Malone advocated that Yao bear down if he wanted to get ahead: "When you come to America, you've got to learn American ways. You're not being a bad guy by learning to play aggressive, by being aggressive even with your own teammates. It's what helps you survive. It's what you need if you want to think about being great."[20]

Even Yao's own teammates encouraged him to assume a more offensive posture. Cuttino Mobley said, "Sometimes you have to turn it on to an aggressive mode where you have to get a little more physical. We told him, . . . we have to tear their head off before they tear ours off."[21] After watching Yao get slapped with his first technical foul for overzealous dunking, Atlanta Hawks 6'10" center Theo Ratliff laughed, "I told Steve [Francis] and Cat Mobley that they're teaching him too much. [Yao] went and got 'Americanized.'"[22]

But Yao had already displayed signs of a killer instinct. After the 2000 Olympics, he was asked which achievement he'd rather have—blocking 30 shots or scoring 30 points. Yao decided, "I'd take the 30 blocks. If you have 30 blocks it will destroy your opponents' morale. It will take away their heart."[23] However, Yao knew better than to take excessive pride in such accomplishments.

According to Sun Tzu, winning is not the ultimate goal. It is merely the predictable outcome of fine-tuning one's ability through careful preparation. Consequently, the appropriate response to a win is not celebration but relief. So after the Rockets notched up a win, Yao waited to exhale, saying, "To get this victory, it's like being able to take a deep breath."[24] By calmly inhaling another lung-full of oxygen, he instinctively did the best thing at the moment: reinvigorate his own "life force."

The Force

For every force there is a counterforce.
Violence, even well intentioned,
always rebounds upon oneself.[25]
—Lao Tzu

Those skilled in the arts of war permit the Spirit of the Heavens to flow within and without themselves.[26]
—Sun Tzu

One can see the relationship between sports and war in the evolution of martial arts. In the Taoist tradition, tai chi and kung fu practitioners incorporated the characteristic behavior of animals into their forms or exercises. Imitating the motion of animals in the wild, leaping in offense, striking in defense, or dodging in evasion, instructors named their schools and styles after creatures such as the monkey, lion, and eagle; motions are known by names like *Grasping the Sparrow's Tail* or *Stepping Back to Ride the Tiger*.

"Tai chi" literally means the "Supreme Ultimate"—the interplay of everything symbolized by the shifting yin and yang. Adherents believe that there is an underlying "life force" that drives all things in the universe. As far-fetched as it sounds, the entertainment series *Star Wars* draws upon this concept, as the old Jedis Obi Wan Kenobi and Yoda teach the "force" to the skeptical youth Luke Skywalker. In the Asian tradition this internal energy is called "chi."

Tai chi's core principle is that people can recognize, track, and harness their own chi as a source of spiritual strength and physical power. Some can sense their chi through the act of breathing and bodily motion. Kareem Abdul-Jabbar attributed his longevity to his adherence to the stretching and weight-lifting regimen taught to him by renowned martial artist Bruce Lee.[27] Others manipulate chi by using techniques like acupuncture, the ancient Chinese healing art where a practitioner inserts a series of thin needles into the patient's body. The goal is to unblock the body's flow of chi, harmonize the functions of its internal organs, and bring its energy back into balance. Plagued with chronic problems to his big toe and back, Shaq has credited his acupuncture treatments for helping him overcome injuries and extend his playing career.[28]

As Yao well knows, keeping one's energy up is a Herculean task given the demands of NBA travel and his mushrooming celebrity. At a morning practice, while his teammates watched idly in the background, Yao was surrounded by a swarm of reporters for the umpteenth time. A question was asked, "How do you maintain your chi?" Stuck in the bleachers, literally cornered by a blockade of microphones, cameras, and tape recorders, Yao smiled resignedly, "I don't think I can anymore."[29]

A skilled martial artist avoids unnecessary confrontation but does not hesitate to harness his chi in self-defense. If one is forced to fight, one must do so on one's own terms and take offense only when necessary. The key is to act at the right time, at the right place, with the right degree of force. By careful observation of the surroundings, one must not be predisposed to action but let it unfold before and into him or her. The master of his own fate is the master of the Tao, doing nothing yet at the same time knowing that something will be done.

Phil Jackson knew the feeling intimately. A 6'8" forward, he was a key reserve on the 1972–73 New York Knicks championship team that starred Earl Monroe, Walt Frazier, Bill Bradley, Dave DeBusschere, and Willis Reed. Two decades later he assembled a machine in Chicago around the nucleus of Michael Jordan and Scottie Pippen, and repeated this trick a decade later in Los Angeles with the tandem of Shaq and Kobe. As a dependable role player, Jackson realized that he had to recruit and motivate athletes who also would to be ready to perform when the opportunity arose.

In a section of his book *Sacred Hoops* entitled "The Tao of Basketball," Phil Jackson called his trademark triangle offense "five-man tai chi." His reason was that, "The basic idea is to orchestrate the flow of movement in order to lure the defense off balance and create a myriad of openings on the floor."[30] Now Yao had to raise his game on both ends of the court to keep pace with the most difficult offenses and defenses he had ever faced.

The Tao of Offense and Defense

Military tacticians have a saying:
'I dare not be the aggressor, but rather the defender;
I dare not advance an inch, but would rather retreat a foot.'
This is to move without moving,
To raise one's fist without showing them,
To lead the enemy on but against no adversary,
To wield a weapon but not clash with the enemy.[31]
—Lao Tzu

Warlords who have mastered defense attack from hidden places
and assure their own success. They know when, where, and how to
make an attack while defending their positions at the same time.[32]
—Sun Tzu

Just as in the golden days of the gridiron, a basketball player still must be able to "go both ways." One must switch between offense and defense at any given moment, with no player substitutions in between. For those watching the flow of the game, the transitions between offense and defense appear seamless. In the blink of an eye, the direction of the possession arrow can change, so one must be ready to shift gears at any time. All five players must be proficient scorers as well as solid defenders to be an effective team. Anyone deficient on either end would soon be exploited as the squad's Achilles heel.

Owning the highest winning percentage of any NBA coach ever for both regular season and playoff games, Phil Jackson knew how to deconstruct an opponent. According to Jackson, the primary advantage of his triangle offense "is that it's based on the Taoist principle of yielding to an opponent's force in order to render him powerless. The idea is not to wilt or act dishonorably in the face of overwhelming force, but to be savvy enough to use the enemy's own power against him. If you look hard enough, you'll find his weakness."[33]

Similarly, Tomjanovich was confident that his new center would be able to find ways for his team to score, saying, "Yao was tremendous inside with moving the ball around, scoring. He puts the defense in a very vulnerable position. If you turn your head and we got guys cutting, you don't know when to help. He's got a great feel for open people. There's no defense that takes away everything. You've got to do one thing or another. You got to do something and there's always an answer and it takes time for guys to learn how to find the answer. He is way ahead of most people coming into the league."[34]

But it wasn't easy for Yao to stay ahead of the curve. The

NBA is a hothouse of evolution, where the survival of the fittest is a constant struggle from game to game. Therefore coaches and players spend long hours dissecting the tendencies of their opponents to find flaws to exploit. Trainers patch the walking wounded. Scouts compile statistics and chart percentages. Assistants pour over film and practice scenarios. Thus, the following running commentary from Yao underscores the constant trials he faces.

> I don't think the defensive speed was tough, but getting back on offense was difficult.[35]

> I played a lot of minutes today. Of course, I want to play more. But I have to build up my endurance. Their defense was very tight on me and I did not have very many opportunities.[36]

> I think the fact their defense on me is getting a lot more active and aggressive shows they respect me more.[37]

> Teams are changing their defenses. I need to work and challenge myself to come out and play better. If they're going to switch their defense, I need to change my offense.[38]

> I'm always thinking about how to improve against the teams and players I'm playing against. What I need to think about most right now is how to deal with different kinds of defenses and how to handle it when defenses adjust during the game.[39]

Tomjanovich was positive that Yao would rise to the occasion, asserting, "We'll probably be seeing some different defenses, but the good thing about Yao is that he's versatile, and if they double-team, he's a great passer. We've gone through some real tough defenses.... What I'm seeing in Yao is that he's versatile, and it's all about the team. If they [opposing defenses] do something to shift some people over, he's going to hit a teammate [with a pass] for an open shot."[40]

A warlord must appear to be all things to all men, but first he must be true to himself and not permit indecisiveness to rule his destiny.[41]
—Sun Tzu

In December 2002 Pete Newell represented the consensus that "[Yao] has been very well taught in back-to-the-basket basketball. His footwork is just excellent for a kid of his size and dimensions. He's an athletic kid, he has a variety of shots.... He's going to get better and better. The players he is playing with have never played with a player like that. They are starting to get the feeling they can go right to the top with this man in the middle, just like the Lakers have done. And they have a right to feel that way."[42]

For both the pretenders and the contenders all routes to the top had to pass through Los Angeles. Soon Yao would have to hit the reigning champs the Lakers head on, and he was already on their radar. The heir apparent to Michael Jordan, the 6'7" dynamo Kobe Bryant, said, "I think it's been great for the game. [Yao's] been a breath of fresh air. He's been able to hold his own, more so than I think people thought."[43] But the biggest roadblock in Yao's path lay right ahead—Kobe's big brother Shaq, the most dominant big man in the game.

At 7'1", and tipping the scales at nearly 350 lbs, Shaquille O'Neal was aptly nicknamed "Diesel." He was a runaway big rig who had only gathered steam since his graduation from Louisiana State University (LSU). The #1 pick of the Orlando Magic, he became the 1992–93 NBA Rookie of the Year, a gold medalist in the 1996 Atlanta Olympics, and nine-time All-Star. Opposing teams had become so desperate that they enacted the infamous strategy of "Hack a Shaq." By intentionally fouling Shaq, they hoped his poor free-throw shooting would drag his team down. In retaliation, the Lakers won three consecutive NBA title rings.

In the meantime Mack Daddy had also gone Hollywood. Using his athletic notoriety as a springboard for even more commercial prominence, Shaq became an eager endorser for everything from soda to shoes. He tried rapping and acting on the silver screen. Among his roles, he played the African American Superman known as *Steel* (living up to the Superman tattoo on his left shoulder), and even posed as a martial arts master in the video game *Shaq-Fu*.

Two months before the season even started, Yao commented on his prospects facing Shaq: "I think it will be one-sided in my match-up against Shaquille O'Neal. He is much better than I at this point. I think the NBA is a very good classroom for me. I think I will learn from defeat and from my setbacks and it will set a foundation for me to improve in the future."[44]

Shaq Attack: War of the Words—and Worlds

Nothing in the world is softer and more supple than water,
Yet when attacking the hard and strong,
nothing can surpass it.
The supple overcomes the hard.
The soft overcomes the strong.[45]

—Lao Tzu

Being resilient is a virtue of the warlord with vision....[46]
—Sun Tzu

The excitement was building for the showdown before Yao stepped foot on American soil. Like King Kong gazing at Godzilla in the distance, Yao looked forward to his first date with Shaq. Scarcely two days after he was drafted, Yao prophesied, "He is a mountain in my way. I will try to conquer it by all means. My first tries may turn out to be failures, but I will continue with others."[47] Two weeks before the season started, Yao reiterated, "Every problem has to be faced. That's going to be a very important game for me. I'm not going to be looking at it as a normal game. I'm going to look at it as a more important game."[48]

A practicing Zen Buddhist, Phil Jackson was known for trying to get into his players' heads. He would give them assigned reading, and once told Shaq to read a book by Friedrich Nietzsche for his "Superman" complex. But there was a method to Jackson's madness. Salon.com wrote, "Jackson has achieved his success with a uniquely New Age approach: a blend of Eastern and Western ideas heretofore

foreign to professional sports. He has been known to regale players with tales of the sacred white buffalo of the plains, coach them in meditation techniques and burn sage to reverse a losing streak.... Indeed, for all the talk of Native American spirituality and Zen, Jackson often displays devilish cruelty. Cruelty is the yin to his New Age yang.... Such is Jackson's way. He demonizes those on the outside to tighten the inner circle."[49]

As it would turn out, due to recurring foot problems (carrying such bulk up and down 94 feet of hardwood was no easy task), Shaq was rehabilitating and missed Yao's first game against the Lakers on November 17, 2002. However, this didn't stop Jackson from firing a shot across Yao's bow: "I feel sorry for the kid. I was hoping it wouldn't be Shaq's first game back, actually. I don't know, [O'Neal] would break him in two. It wouldn't be fair for the kid to go against Shaquille, such a dominant force, such a dynamic amount of energy."[50] Nevertheless, boosted by Yao's 20 points, the Rockets triumphed and set the stage for the next time, when both big men would finally square off.

When informed of his coach's bragging on his behalf, "Big Aristotle" responded, "Would I break him in two? Con-

---

Water meets the rock, Shaquille O'Neal.

"Empty your mind, be formless, shapeless—like water. Now you put water into a cup, it becomes the cup. You put water into a bottle, it becomes the bottle.

"You put it in a teapot, it becomes the teapot. Now water can flow or it can crash! Be water, my friend."

—Bruce Lee

gratulations to Mr. Ming, first of all. He's done a lot for his country. Whenever you have a guy that comes in like that, you must take it to him before he takes it to you. He has all the tools. He can shoot. He can dribble. He's no slouch."[51]

But belying this nonchalance, just a few months earlier Shaq had shown a vastly different face to the press. Shaq would later regret ever having taken this derisive stance. Once sparked by Shaq's incendiary remarks, the hype over their upcoming game together would blast into hyperdrive.

Insult the enemy with subtlety where and when you can insult him; degrade where and when you can degrade. Offer fool's bait and entice him to display his stupidity. Do something that may appear stupid and capitalize on his arrogance.[52]

—Sun Tzu

On June 28, 2002, Shaquille O'Neal had taunted Yao and LA Clippers center Wang Zhi Zhi on Fox Television's boorish cable TV program *The Best Damn Sports Show Period.* When the subject of Yao Ming was brought up, Shaq, in a bogus Chinese accent, blustered, "Tell Yao Ming, 'ching-chong-yang-wah-ah-soh.'"[53] Making phony kung fu moves, he continued, "I look forward to breaking down that mother———'s body. He said my name three times, two in Chinese and one in American. You don't ever call me out. I'm from LSU."[54] Amazingly, no one said a peep about it. However, O'Neal's summertime slur was then repeatedly, and tactlessly, replayed on December 16 and 17, 2002, by Tony Bruno, host of the *Morning Extravaganza* on Fox Sports Radio.[55] A columnist for

AsianWeek, Irwin Tang, revived the story, and soon Shaq's words ignited a media firestorm. Controversy is music to a reporter's ears, and a running conversation between both men ensued in the pages of newspapers from coast to coast. Asked about his reaction, Yao stated, "I really only found out about it in the last two days. I think there are a lot of difficulties in two different cultures understanding each other, especially countries of very large populations [such as] China and the United States. The world is getting smaller and has a greater understanding of cultures. I believe Shaquille O'Neal was joking with what he said, but I think a lot of Asian people don't understand this kind of joke."[56]

When questioned whether O'Neal should apologize, Yao replied: "I think that's something he'll have to decide ... for himself." Then Yao made light of the incident, saying, "Chinese is hard to learn. Even when I was little, I took a long time to learn Chinese."[57]

A meek Phil Jackson downplayed the incident that suddenly cast his superstar in a most unfavorable light. "It's an unfortunate situation. I'm sure that Shaq had no meaning like that behind it. I'm sure he was just doing something that was fun-loving or something he thought was humorous."[58]

> *The simplest way to humble, humiliate, and debase your enemy is to cut him off from his supplies.*[59]
>
> —Sun Tzu

Even so, fans and writers worldwide quickly began trying Shaq's case in the court of public opinion. Soon it became clear, even to Shaq, that the tide of popular sentiment had turned against him. He could no longer even count on support from his home base, the Laker faithful and local media. But still Shaq claimed it wasn't his fault if people didn't appreciate his humor or accept his remorse.

> Over my 11 years in the NBA, I know for a fact that most of you guys are going to write what you want to write, and it's our job to either defend it or just let it go. At times I try to be a comedian. Sometimes I make a good joke and sometimes it's a bad joke. That's just the ups and downs of trying to be a comedian.[60]

> I said it jokingly, so this guy was just trying to stir something up that's not there. He's just somebody who doesn't have a sense of humor, like I do. I don't have to have a response to [the charges of racism] because the people who know me know I'm not. I mean, if I was the first one to do it, and the only one to do it, I could see what they're talking about. But if I offended anybody, I apologize.[61]

> To say I'm a racist against Asians is crazy. It's probably [someone] just trying to start trouble.... I'm an idiot prankster. I said a joke. It was a 70–30 joke. Seventy percent of people thought it was funny, 30 didn't. At times I try to be a comedian. Sometimes I say good jokes, sometimes I say bad jokes. If I hurt anybody's feelings, I apologize.[62]

> Toy-inchee. Chinese for "I'm sorry." For when I see Yao Ming.[63]

THE TAO OF YAO

In the fall of 1990, Bill Walton was hired by LSU coach Dale Brown to tutor the sophomore Shaq for five days.[64] However, a decade later Walton was plainly disappointed in Shaq's lack of maturity. Prior to gameday, Walton added his two cents: "The recent release of recordings of Shaquille O'Neal mocking, criticizing and generally disrespecting Yao Ming are startling. How disappointing for Shaq—he should know better. He's the leader of the NBA and you expect more from him. Can you imagine Bill Russell, Michael Jordan, Larry Bird, Magic, Hakeem or David Robinson saying anything like this?"[65] Walton continued, "If Shaq were your 10-year-old child, what would you do or say to him? What if Yao had said something about Shaq's ethnicity? Imagine the outcry. There is no place in this world for Shaq's intolerance and insensitivity. If this is what he is saying publicly, imagine what he's saying privately. As far as Shaq's 'apology' is concerned, I don't get it when someone says, 'If I offended anyone, I'm sorry.' That tactic worked really well for Trent Lott. How many times can a man turn his head, pretending he just doesn't see?"[66]

As both the attention and pressure continued to mount from all sides, Jackson spelled out the obvious: "I think a lot of the focus is due to the controversy because some people took umbrage to Shaq's remarks. I can't remember a matchup with Shaq that is comparable."[67]

Game Faces

So when opposing armies clash,
the compassionate
are the ones who win.[68]

—Lao Tzu

A true warlord never lets his sword be out of reach. He keeps it
close because he is aware of the calamities that can destroy him:
imprudence, cowardice, belligerance, arrogance, and charity.[69]

—Sun Tzu

As the duel on January 17, 2003, drew near, Lakers guard Kobe Bryant said that winning the game was his most important concern. "With the fact that we have to win this game, the hype around Yao Ming is kind of secondary. But [Shaq] is going to be ready to play.... Personally, I think it's unfair to Yao Ming. He's nowhere close to Shaquille O'Neal. But it's going to be an enjoyable game."[70]

Contemplating his upcoming encounter with Shaq the next day, Yao tried to find common ground, somewhere between humor and hyperbole:

I've already gone through a lot of tests and this is going to be one of the most difficult ones.[71]

It seems to me that physically I may still be lacking a little bit [to match up equally]. I think I need a suit of armor for Friday night.[72]

I think [Shaq] has a lot of meat on his elbows, so maybe it won't hurt that much.... [Shaq] is always smiling and is a very happy person. I think he lives a very happy life.... This is a very important reason that factored into my decision to come into the NBA. The game will be a little different than a normal game.... I don't think there's any animosity. We're all basketball players. We all live together on this Earth.[73]

In his defense Shaq fired back, "I know I can take it to guys bigger than me. Playing a shot-blocker brings out the best in me, so I'm looking forward to playing him. I don't have to outscore him to solidify my position in this game. Everybody knows who I am. In America, in China, Africa, they all know who I am."[74]

Now, if you attack with kindness, you will be victorious; if you defend yourself with it, you will be impregnably solid.[75]

—Lao Tzu

In war it is essential to make the enemy think one thing while you deliver a strike from another direction. It is essential to keep the enemy off balance, even by feigning assistance to him. Make him think you are befriending him while you plan his demise.[76]

—Sun Tzu

To the surprise of many, Yao offered Shaq an invitation to dinner at his Houston home the night before the big game.

However Shaq, declined Yao's offer and the chance to sample his mom's cooking. Instead Shaq chose to visit his six-year-old daughter and her mother in Houston. When asked why O'Neal had said no, Yao guessed, "I don't think our refrigerator is big enough."[77]

Then before the game, Yao would get some moral support from some friendly figures. Hakeem Olajuwon counseled, "All Yao needs is reassurance and that comes from just going out there and playing against Shaq. He knows that he has the tools. It is doing it, even if he fails at first, that will give him the reassurance." Seated next to the Dream while watching the game, Moses Malone professed, "Yao is just next. MVP to MVP to MVP. That's the way it should be."[78]

Subsequently, during a pre-game photo op with Olajuwon and Malone, Shaq reputedly whispered to Yao, "I love you, we're friends." Later Yao would kid, "I thought of reminding him he just got married."[79]

The buzz at the Compaq Center was palpable. A reported 16,285 fans jammed into the stadium, eager to see the drama unfold on the court (one of ten sellouts during the season vs. three the year before). In this case, the game did live up to expectations and then some. Again the Rockets won, but this time eked out a 108–104 decision in overtime. Steve Francis stole the show with a career-high 44 points, and he fed Yao for a game-clinching slam. Afterwards Kobe affirmed, "Shaq was up for the game. It took him some time to adjust to [Yao's] size but once he did, it was back to the boom."[80] Indeed, Shaq piled up 31 points and 13 rebounds against Yao's 10 points and 10 rebounds.

But Yao registered six blocks and rejected Shaq three times in the first breathtaking minutes of play. Lakers coach Phil Jackson reluctantly admitted of Yao, "He got some credibility in this game."[81]

For his part, Yao was glad to have survived. To him Shaq was "like a meat wall."[82] If that comparison wasn't clear enough, Yao elaborated, "He's like a truck. I've never encountered someone that strong before. He's not crafty, it's just strength. It wore me out playing him."[83] But after the dust settled, Yao knew that he had achieved more than just a moral victory: "It gave me great encouragement. I felt like I was underwater for a long time and now I can finally breathe."[84]

In the locker room after the game, Shaq again tried to defuse the racial controversy he created while taking a swipe at his detractors. To probing reporters, he retorted,

I already apologized in Los Angeles. And I just want to say this: Yao Ming is my brother, the Asian people are my brothers, I have an Asian doctor. It's just unfortunate that an idiot writer [in *Asian Week*] would try to start a racial war when there's really nothing there. I said a joke, maybe it was funny, maybe it wasn't funny. I already apologized. But an idiot writer from a small paper started it, and I'm surprised that some of you big guys [in the media], rather than just sticking to the facts, that you jumped on the bandwagon. So I'm disappointed in some of you media people for that. And that's why sometimes I don't talk to you. Because if you're going to be a writer, sit your [butt] down and write. Don't make [stuff] up, and don't try to start nothing.[85]

The aftershocks of the heavyweight fight were felt far and wide. *The New York Times* concluded, "If O'Neal could just step back from the bravado, view the game from Yao's perch of perspective, he might pick up some valuable pointers on composure, open-mindedness, and leadership.... While O'Neal loses his poise like car keys, Yao has shown remarkable composure for a battered big man on the spot. From Day 1, he has been a self-effacing, punch-line wiz who craves acceptance but shares his wisdom."[86]

Yet again, O'Neal tried to put the situation into a more palatable perspective: "I grew up an Army kid. I grew up around Asians, around whites, around browns. It was a bad joke. Don't try to make a racial war out of it. Because of what I said, 500 million people saw this game. You ought to thank me for my marketing skills."[87]

On that score, Shaq happened to be right on the money. Afterwards ESPN proudly announced that the game's 3.82 household rating was its highest ever for a basketball program, making it the second most-viewed regular-season game in cable television history.[88] The first was shortly after Magic Johnson came out of retirement after being diagnosed as HIV (Human Immunodeficiency Virus, the cause of AIDS) positive; in Magic's second game back, the Lakers suited up against Michael Jordan's Chicago Bulls on February 2, 1996.[89] Following those hallowed memories, Yao and Shaq were destined to have blockbuster sequels. Ironically the next time would be scarcely a month later, when they would actually be on the same side.

Stars and Stripes

A man with outward courage dares to die. A man with inward courage dares to live.[90]

—Lao Tzu

War does not permit faltering personal belief.[91]

—Sun Tzu

Adding another twist to Yao and Shaq's incipient rivalry, simmering controversy now moved to the front burner. Which man would (and should) be chosen as the Western Conference's starting center for the upcoming 2003 All-Star game? The NBA had decided to accommodate international fans by allowing them to vote in Spanish and Chinese on its website, also providing instructions in seven other languages. Yet this global marketing ploy had its critics. On national television, ABC sportscaster Brent Musburger feared that "the hordes of China" would tilt the All-Star voting toward Yao instead of Shaq.[92]

Soon it became apparent that the world's balance of basketball power had shifted. The running tally showed that Yao was leading the balloting over Shaq. To this surprising turn of events, Yao said, "There are two sides to it, making the All-Star team. On one side, it would be a great encouragement to me, but on the other side it would be just more pressure. If I make it, I just hope to have some fun.... I'm very honored by the voting. I'm sure a lot of it is my countrymen [in China] voting for me."[93] As the meaning of it began to sink in, Yao responded in his typical blend of wit, practicality, and modesty:

> [Describing wide-eyed astonishment and open-mouthed awe at the voting results]
> My eyes seem to be bigger than my mouth, and my mouth seems to be bigger than a bicycle tire.[94]

> Shaq is a great player who has proved his domination of the game. Of course, it makes me very happy to have the support of my country. That people in China can vote for the NBA All-Star Game on the Internet is another example of how small the world is becoming.[95]

> [Shaq's] the best center in the game. Why can't he start and I come off the bench?[96]

For his part Shaq appeared nonchalant about being overshadowed. "It happens to the best of us," he said. "When I came in, I beat out Patrick Ewing. . . . He [Yao] is making history for his people. His people are proud of him. They should be. One billion people—that's tough to beat."[97]

Once the polls were closed and the ballots tabulated, Yao made history again. With 814,393 votes to Shaq's 655,744, Yao became the 16th rookie in history to start in the All-Star game, and the first international first-year player to do so. Of his official stature Yao said, "I'm very honored and hope I play well in the game. I think I might have to take sleeping pills before I can go to sleep tonight. To have this opportunity makes me very happy. This is a rare opportunity."[98]

THE TAO OF YAO

But this was a bitter pill for Shaq to swallow, especially since he was the MVP of three straight NBA championship teams. Later when asked what would he tell his kids about the results, Shaq released his frustration: "The only way to beat your daddy in the All-Stars was they had to open it up in China."[99] He elaborated,

> It's just a matter of mathematics. The town he's from [Shanghai] has about 18 million people. And me? I'm from North San Antonio and Orlando and Los Angeles, and together they don't have 18 million. So, mathematically speaking, wasn't no way I was going to win. But I'll win in the end. I just think it's unfair the way they did the voting. If they are going to open up the computer voting to all those billions of people in China, then why didn't they do the same for Germany and for Africa and for all over the world? I don't like that, but promoting Yao is good for the game. . . . It really doesn't matter whether I start for the All-Star team because I've done it many times before. All I'm interested in now is winning championships.[100]

And it wasn't over yet. Reporters still hounded Yao about his thoughts from every conceivable angle. When asked if Shaq would play more than him in the upcoming All-Star game, Yao fired back a culinary metaphor: "I really don't know. It's just like, how will you know the taste of the Szechuan spicy dish before eating it?"[101] Responding to whether he would surrender his starting spot to Shaq, just like Tracy McGrady and Allen Iverson had volunteered for the retiring Michael Jordan (who politely declined), Yao asserted, "This is a rare chance that I cannot give up. You have to understand that there are some differences between the starting center and the back-up center in the NBA. A good center needs strength and skills, and all of you can see for yourself which of the two centers is better."[102]

Still trying to smooth things over, Shaq complimented Yao by saying, "He's very good for the league. And I'm a connoisseur of what's good for the league."[103] But he couldn't resist sticking it to his new rival when he picked another horse to win Rookie of the Year. "Right now, I'd still say it's my guy, Amare Stoudemire [forward for the Phoenix Suns]. Don't get me wrong. Yao is good. Damn good. But Stoudemire is already dominating more guys who have been in the league for several years, and he's going to get much better. Yao is dominating, too. But he caught me off guard the first time I played him. I'll know how to play him better from here on out. Other guys will figure him out, too."[104]

After all the talk, Yao must have been relieved to leap for the jump ball on February 9, 2003, when the All-Star game finally commenced. But the double-overtime thriller belonged to Kevin Garnett who scored 37, helped the West win 155–145, and took home the MVP award. Jordan notched 20 and passed Kareem Abdul-Jabbar as the All-Star game's career leading scorer. Meanwhile, Shaq chipped in 19 points and 13 rebounds. As part of the only pair of team-mates to start, Houston's Steve Francis tallied 20 points and 9 assists as well. Although he made the only shot he attempted, Yao was pleased to be there in the first place: "It was a lot of fun tonight. It was like attending a party. I didn't mind the lack of playing time. It's just something that makes everybody happy and gives people something to watch.... Of course, I wouldn't mind playing more. But I think in the future I'll have more of an opportunity."[105]

Undoubtedly he will. In the NBA, rivalries can quickly develop as teams play each other many times a season, and dozens of times over the span of players' careers. The next game is just the next chapter. In their rematch on March 26, 2003, the Compaq Center enjoyed its tenth and final sell-out of Yao's season. But Shaq dominated Yao (39 points, 5 rebounds versus 6 points, 10 rebounds) and the Lakers won 96–93. After winning this round, Shaq bragged that he still owned the collar of the top dog: "I took it away from Hakeem [Olajuwon] a couple years ago when he decided to leave, so now it's mine. And you have to outplay me at least a couple years before I give you the M.D.E. [Most Dominant Ever] title."[106]

Subtly arrange the outcome and nothing more.
Do not force.
After the outcome do not be complacent.
After the outcome do not be smug.
After the outcome do not be conceited.
Overcome only because there is no other alternative.
Overcome but do not force.[107]

—Lao Tzu

When a conflict is completed, the warlord should be in the position of controlling the state from the attitude of a higher viewpoint.[108]

—Sun Tzu

Basketball games are a series of skirmishes in an ongoing war. After all was said and done, Yao was asked, "Are you and Shaq friends now?" Yao simply replied, "Not on the court."[109] Knowing firsthand how easily the media can cook up jealousy as well as amity, Bill Russell took pains to debunk the theory that he disliked his most famous nemesis:

> Wilt Chamberlain and I carried on a friendship the entire time we played basketball together, even though the newspapers portrayed us as mortal enemies. There's a certain amount of show business in professional basketball, and the two of us were a promoter's dream.... Offhand I can't think of any two players in a team sport who have been cast as antagonists and as personifications of various theories more than Wilt and I were. Almost any argument people wanted to have could be carried on in the Russell vs. Chamberlain debate, and almost any virtue and sin was imagined to be at stake. If we weren't a metaphor for something, we were at least a symbol of it.[110]

So too Yao and Shaq became flashpoints for the culture at large. Taking the high road, Yao refused to be driven by hubris. Instead, by defending his position, Yao let his opponent make the first ill-fated move. Instead of gaining respect, Shaq lost face. Standing up for himself, Yao and his capable conduct made his diverse constituency of supporters proud.

*The softest things in the world overcome the hardest things in the
    world.*
Through this I know the advantage of taking no action.[111]
                        —Lao Tzu

According to Lao, this softness is the epitome of "non-doing."
Stephen Mitchell explains, "Softness means the opposite of
rigidity, and is synonymous with suppleness, adaptability,
endurance. Anyone who has seen a tai chi or aikido master
doing not-doing will know how powerful this softness is."[112]
In this early clash of the titans, Yao displayed a maturity that
belied his young age. At the same time he exemplified the
qualities of a warrior in a long-standing tradition of wisdom.

九 9

Being in the Center

We join spokes together in a wheel,
but it is the center hole
that makes the wagon move.[1]

—Lao Tzu

I will try to grab as many rebounds as I can, do my best to
provide strong support to our outside players. That's what a center
should do.[2]

—Yao Ming

If a basketball team can be considered a hand, then each of the five starters is a finger. Though a proud point guard would disagree, the center is considered the thumb. Traditionally the center is the biggest and best player on both ends of the court. It is the pivot that makes the offense function—the default choice and fail-safe option. It is the glue

---

"Who is this rare bird, perched at the eerie dead center of the world's hurricane, whom all men delight to praise?"[3]

—Alistair Cooke

that holds the defense together—the shot blocker and last line of protection.

One of the first players to go "hardship," Moses Malone became a two-time league MVP and the fifth-leading scorer and rebounder in NBA history. Named one of the greatest 50 players in 1996, Malone had his #24 jersey retired by the Rockets in 1998 and lumbered into the Hall of Fame in 2001. Drawing from a 21-year career as a steadfast center, now Moses advised Yao: "It's the big man in the middle who makes it all go. Think about when I was playing in the NBA, when Dream was playing. You know what those other guys were always hearing from us out on the floor: 'Give me the ball!' There are a lot of nights when your big man's got to get 20 to 25 shots a game. That's how you win championships."[4]

Each successive generation of giants has defined and redefined the game. George Mikan. Bill Russell. Walt Bellamy. Nate Thurmond. Wilt Chamberlain. Willis Reed. Wes Unseld. Dave Cowens. Robert Parish. Patrick Ewing. Once feared like the Tyrannosaurus Rex, the center was king of all he surveyed. Yet today their reign is on the wane and their members are a vanishing species, so there has been much speculation around the decline of the center. Back in a 1993 interview with *The Washington Post*, rising center Alonzo Mourning explained why his job had fewer applicants: "Elbows are flying, people pushing, barking. You're up in people's breath. It's not too pleasant down there in the hole. That's why only a select few play down there.... A lot of people get big bucks, but very rarely do you find people that want to go down there and put up with that, night in and night out. I'm one of the select few who do."[5]

No longer does a player's size dictate their position. Pete Newell ran the numbers. "If you look at the fellows playing center, 60 percent will score 10 or less points," he said. "That implies that center is not the focal point. Center was once considered the position."[6] Following the 1980s example of Ralph Sampson, a new generation of athletic big men has evolved to play further from the basket at the expense of their control over the offensive flow. Houston coach Rudy Tomjanovich said, "Every era had somebody who stretched the boundaries of talent in the league. But I never imagined the size, strength and agility of the guys playing today."[7]

This is especially true for those players from abroad, where there is a higher premium placed on overall skills such as ball-handling and footwork. Exemplified by Dirk Nowitzki, seven-footers are as likely to shoot three-pointers as clog the lane. When Kiki Vandeweghe was the Mavericks' director of player development, he instructed Yao when the Chinese national team had a summer training session in Dallas. Vandeweghe reported, "Looking around Europe and the world, they play a different style. The center position is more important to the way they want to play there. The game is global now; you're never going to stop that."[8]

Before his rematch with Yao, Shaq conferred another label of "Most Dominant" on himself, boasting, "I'm the M.D. I'll be the M.D. for 10 years."[9] Though he was considered an underachiever until he became a Laker and was joined by Kobe Bryant and guru Phil Jackson, since then Shaq had chalked up three straight titles and cemented his legacy as an impact player. As Newell noted, "Shaq, when he retires, will go down as one of the greatest centers."[10] Modestly,

Shaq agreed by also referring to himself as "LCL," the Last Center Left. Shaq predicted, "I'm the last of the true centers. After I leave, there won't be any more."[11]

However, for as long as Shaq was around, other teams would have to find ways to deal with him or face the consequences. "Twenty years ago, it was Kareem [Abdul-Jabbar], now it's Shaq," says Scott Lloyd, a former NBA center working for the Dallas Mavericks. "Everyone wants a dominant big man because it's the only way to get past the Lakers."[12] Acknowledging this predicament, Steve Francis was suddenly optimistic about the Rockets' future: "You're not going very far in this league without a big man. And now we have one."[13]

Adding Yao made it a whole new ball game for Houston, attested Michael Jordan: "[Yao] plugged a lot of big holes that [the Rockets] had last year in terms of productivity in that center spot. And defensively, he can definitely block shots and plug up that center position. It's going to help them a whole lot because they have the perimeter guys and they just needed that big figure in the center."[14] Philadelphia's General Manager for twelve years, Pat Williams had traded for Julius Erving and then Moses Malone to bring the 76ers the 1983 title. Having drafted Charles Barkley and later Shaquille O'Neal for the Orlando Magic, Williams appraised the Rockets' new center: "Ewing, Sampson and Walton came in with a lot of flourish, but nothing quite like this guy. This is amazing. This is the real deal."[15]

Pete Newell always had a keen appreciation for talented big men. As the Lakers' General Manager, Newell brokered the blockbuster deal in 1975 that brought Kareem Abdul-

© The Sporting News

🔺 The Big Fella rising over Houston's Ralph Sampson.

"Kareem [Abdul-Jabbar] was probably, with his size and his sky hook, the most dominating force in our league as far as getting a basket any time you want it."[16]

—Larry Bird

Jabbar from the hinterland of Milwaukee (where he won a title with Oscar Robertson in 1971) to Los Angeles. Soon thereafter Newell started his "Big Man Camp," which became the best-kept secret of the modern age of professional coaching. There he taught hundreds of players who wanted to improve their skills, from collegiates and journeymen, to stars (Kareem, Walton, Shaq, Divac), forwards (Scottie Pippen, Antawn Jamison, Kenyon Martin), and raw rookies (Tyson Chandler, Kwame Brown, Eddie Curry). Newell observed that even Hakeem didn't start his NBA career with twinkle toes:

> Probably the biggest drawback for most big players is that they are not conscious of their left foot, and as a result, they never develop it. We call them one-foot players. Shaq was like that when he first showed up. But like Hakeem, he wanted badly to learn. It's funny, when [Houston coach] Bill Fitch sent Hakeem to us in 1984, he had no moves at all. What he had was the ambidexterity of the feet. I remember asking him, "Who taught you to move your feet like that?" He said, "Coach, no one teach me. I play soccer."
>
> So what you see in Hakeem now, he's not going to talk about it, but in his mind, you can't stop him because he has too many moves, too many ways to beat you.[17]

Newell brightened up when thinking about the prospects for Yao as well as for the position in general, commenting, "Every time I see him, I'm amazed. He shows every indication of being taught the game. I think the game will rediscover the big fellows, but not until the high school coaches begin to teach. But so many coaches never were exposed to teaching. What are they going to do?"[18]

The Anti-Center

Whether you go up the ladder or down it,
your position is shaky.
When you stand with your two feet on the ground,
you will always keep your balance.[19]

—Lao Tzu

Recently calling tai chi "the perfect exercise" since it "builds strength, agility, and best of all balance," *Time* magazine explained, "Practitioners praise Tai Chi's spiritual and psychological benefits, but what has attracted the attention of Western scientists lately is what Tai Chi does for the body. In many ways, researchers are just catching up to what tens of millions of people in China and Chinatowns around the rest of the world already know about Tai Chi."[20]

In tai chi, practitioners begin their exercise by "centering" their chi. Contrary to what Westerners think, jutting out one's chest and shoulders is not the best stance to be ready for action. A US Marine would be better prepared by loosening his belly. With the knees relaxed and feet shoulder width apart, one "holds the center" by shifting weight to the hips and abdomen. There one feels one's center of gravity, right below the navel. From this firm but flexible foundation, one strings together a series of coordinated movements. Being centered means being grounded. Being grounded means being balanced. Therefore a centered person starts from a position of strength to dynamically respond in any direction.

As Houston's center, Yao represents a new type of big man. Surely, as the hub around which the Rockets revolve, he is the linchpin for both the offense and the defense. Yet in a Taoist sense, he symbolizes the "anti-center." Embodying the qualities of water, he is fluid as much as fixed. To benefit his comrades he is willing to transparently work behind the scenes as much as grab attention as the front man. Selfless to the last, Yao said, "Of course, the thing that hurts me the most is when I can't contribute to the team."[21]

Though he initially stuck out like a sore thumb, Yao downplayed his physical stature. When asked about his tendency to settle for jumpshots at the 2002 World Basketball Championships, Yao explained, "First of all, I'm not buff enough. I got pushed away from the basket. And even when I didn't, I couldn't get anyone to throw me a pass."[22] However, he neglected to mention how he roughed up Team Canada a few weeks earlier on August 16th in Vancouver. Though China lost 94–66, Yao broke forward Andrew Kwiatkowski's wrist while going for a rebound, and later bruised Prosper Karangwa's ribs so severely that the guard was forced to wear a flak jacket for the remainder of the tournament.

Directing Team USA at Indianapolis, George Karl, coach of the Milwaukee Bucks, owned up to how Yao quickly made a believer of him and his players: "His size is very intimidating, both defensively and his ability to shoot and pass over people. I think he'll get better and better. You're going to have to get near his shot to make him miss it and that's a very difficult thing to do. . . . No question he was a major factor around the basket. Offensively it looks like he's going to be very difficult to be covered. It looks like he always will be able to shoot and get over the top of you. His size reminds me of Wilt Chamberlain's size when Wilt Chamberlain had a lot of size on people."[23]

At 7'1", 275 lbs, Chamberlain played like a man among boys during his entire career. Teammate Jerry West said, "Wilt was so dominant that it was almost a joke to watch other players play against him."[24] Famed for many exploits, Chamberlain was the only man to score 100 points in one game, and he averaged an unprecedented 50 points a game during the 1961–62 season, rewriting the record books in the process. The Big Dipper was so awesome that the NBA changed many rules to give his opponents a fighting chance, such as widening the lane, calling offensive goaltending, and shooting free throws from a standing position (since Wilt would jump toward the basket and lay the ball in). Retiring at the early age of 36 in 1974, Wilt said, "Everybody pulls for David, nobody roots for Goliath."

Once in the NBA, Yao anticipated facing the stilt-like 7'6" Dallas center Shawn Bradley for a few reasons: "I don't get many chances to play against a player as tall as me, so I was very excited. I know I'm not the skinniest player in the NBA."[25] However, others saw Yao differently. Minnesota Timberwolves coach Flip Saunders said, "He's the second-best center in the league already, all things considered. Offensively, he's got a lot of skill, and once he gets the ball down low, it's over. He already changes the way you have to play."[26]

Minnesota Timberwolves TV analyst Mychal Thompson appreciated this fact. Graduating from the University of Minnesota with Flip Saunders, the 6'10" Bahamian was chosen #1 in the 1977–78 draft by the Portland Trail Blazers to fill the void left by Bill Walton. Later Thompson rounded out his career in Los Angeles by helping Kareem and Magic win back-to-back championships in 1986 and 1987. Now Thompson gave Yao the ultimate compliment: "I tell you, man, he can be as good as Kareem Abdul-Jabbar in that low post because of his unselfishness, his willingness to help out his teammates. I just don't understand why the Rockets have taken this long to figure out you run your offense through Yao Ming."[27]

However, it did take time for Kareem to develop his own offensive repertoire. It may surprise fans to know that the NCAA actually outlawed dunking in 1967. Attending UCLA during this period, Abdul-Jabbar was forced to experiment and rely on other shots. Under Wooden's watchful eye, soon Kareem developed his signature weapon. Never since duplicated or rivaled, Kareem's sky hook was regal, rhythmic, and relentless. Through the years of sheer repetition of making baskets in practice, Kareem concluded, "Shooting is a very Zen activity. You center on your inner calm and your target, isolating everything else until you and your objective become one."[28]

Explaining why the center is the keystone of the team:
"That's just basketball. That's not me. That's the position."[29]

—Hakeem Olajuwon

THE TAO OF YAO

Yao seems to possess this gift of concentration and talent. According to Dirk Nowitzki, "Yao isn't like most big men who basically stay in one place. He's all over the court. The best thing is his shooting touch. He's got a soft jump hook and his 15- to 16-foot jumper ... it's money. Once he gets adjusted to the NBA and the lifestyle in America, he's going to be awesome."[30] ESPN's Bill Simmons concurred, adding, "Exceptionally well schooled and mobile, [Yao] affects the game at both ends like nobody since Bill Walton. His turn-around jumper—a borderline work of art—might be the most unblockable move since Kareem's skyhook."[31]

When asked to pick his favorite move, Yao deadpanned, "I like to shoot the ball and have it go in. I don't like to shoot and not have it go in."[32] Just two months into his rookie year, Yao was on a torrid pace. Over a six-game stretch from November 9 to 21, he made more than 88% of his shots (31 of 35). In the process he broke Wilt's NBA record of field goal percentage for six consecutive games, a mark that had stood since 1966.

Appropriately, Hakeem's number #34 was retired by Houston on November 9, 2002, two years after his college teammate Drexler's #22. The NBA's all-time leader with 3,830 blocked shots, Olajuwon was a twelve-time All-Star, five-time All-Defensive Team selection, and one of just eight players with 20,000 points and 12,000 rebounds. A month later, Houston coach Rudy Tomjanovich reflected, "Yao is so inspiring. It just gives me goose bumps sometimes after he makes a play, to hear that buzz in the crowd, people saying, 'Could you believe that?' It was reminiscent of when Dream [Olajuwon] was here."[33]

On Hakeem's retirement, Yao said, "I've seen him for a long time, and I've learned a lot of things from watching him. I knew this day would come, and I am sorry that it has. I hope he can come to Houston and become a coach and teach me more."[34] When asked if he would ever imitate Olajuwon's famous move "The Dream Shake," Yao demurred, "I'd probably fall over."[35] However, as one of the 50 Greatest Players in NBA history in 1996 and a Hall of Famer, Hakeem encouragingly said of Yao, "With his height and competitiveness, this guy has unlimited potential to raise the bar to another level."[36]

Likewise, opponents were quick to recognize Yao's ability: "He's a smart basketball player," said Tracy McGrady. "You see that right away. It's not just his moves, it's that he knows where to go when he's double-teamed. To be honest, I don't think they give him the ball enough right now. I wish I had a guy like that—a guy inside who can open things up outside. He deserved to be an All-Star. He'll be there every year, for a long, long time."[37]

Destined for the Hall of Fame after his retirement as McGrady's teammate in 2002, 7'0" Patrick Ewing was an eleven-time All-Star and named one of the NBA's Top 50 players ever. Before joining his former coach Jeff Van Gundy as a Rockets' assistant coach for the 2003–04 season, Ewing said of Yao, "He should be the next dominant center after Shaquille. His upside is great."[38] Having coached McGrady as well as his former New York Knicks teammate Ewing in his final year, the Orlando Magic's Doc Rivers bemoaned, "[Yao] is going to be a great, great, great player in this league. He can do so many things. I'm jealous because

Houston gets so many great centers. When are we going to get one?"[39]

Given all that had been said and written about him, there was no substitute for seeing Yao in person. His impressive performance against the Golden State Warriors on March 21, 2003, symbolized how far he'd come as a center and how much farther he could go. In front of a full house of 20,193 fans (the largest attendance in Warriors' history), Yao lost the opening tip but was the Rockets' leading scorer in the first quarter. Scoring on a variety of moves, Yao made jump shots, hooks, lay-ups, and follow-up dunks. At times he was bowled over by Warriors relentlessly driving to the basket. At other moments, he blocked four shots and altered many into airballs. But as the fourth quarter drew near a close, his teammates fed Yao the ball, knowing he'd be fouled immediately. Coolly Yao sank four straight free throws to ice the win and then swished his first and only three-pointer of the year for good measure, as Houston won 117–107. Sitting out the entire second quarter, Yao finished with 23 points and 14 rebounds, leaving few skeptics behind as the crowd filed out.

Jeff Van Gundy said, "With the new rules in the NBA, it's much more difficult to play the post-up game. But when I see him every game, he's a little bit better. That goes to his upbringing, his culture and his demeanor. He has enough humility to say, 'I don't know everything. I can get better.' That's why he's going to be an absolute star. His combination of humility, humor and competitiveness—it's remarkable. I love the guy."[40]

Afterwards in the Warriors' post-game press conference,

Yao was asked the following question: "At the end of the game, when the score was close, your teammates really relied on you to secure the victory. Were you pleased with that?" Yao answered, "I like that feeling a lot. But it was very dangerous. If we had played a little better, it probably wouldn't have been like that."[41] Even in triumph, Yao instinctively balanced his satisfaction with that of his team's: he was happy to demonstrate his worth, but wanted Houston to improve as well. In the center of a storm of pressure and expectations, Yao was calm. With both feet firmly on the ground, Yao would prove to be the heart of Houston's turnaround.

The Master sees things as they are,
without trying to control them.
He lets them go their own way,
and resides at the center of the circle.[42]

—Lao Tzu

"The self-explorer, whether he wants to or not, becomes the explorer of everything else. He learns to see himself, but suddenly, provided he was honest, all the rest appears, and it is as rich as he was, and, as a final crowning, richer."[1]

—Elias Canetti

THE TAO OF YAO

Chapter 10

Lighting the Way

If you open yourself to insight,
you are at one with insight
and you can use it completely.[2]

　　　　　　　　—Lao Tzu

I will have my value recognized in several years.[3]
　　　　　　　　—Yao Ming

Charles Barkley fondly retold a recent joke by comedian Chris Rock: "You know the world is off tilt when the best rapper is a white guy, the best golfer is a black guy, the tallest basketball player is Chinese, and Germany doesn't want to go to war."

Perhaps the Earth had been turned upside down. But at least Yao's basketball revolution would delight fans across the globe. Before he ever played an NBA minute, Yao graced the cover of *Sports Illustrated*. The feature story for *SI*'s annual NBA Preview issue was "The New Mr. Big," which cautiously concluded, "The best guess here is that [Yao] will spend the next couple of years learning from the league's diversified big men, then spend the rest of his career taking them to school."[4]

> "Perhaps the most remarkable thing about China's tallest ambassador is that he is possibly even more popular in the U.S. than he is at home.... Yao's appeal transcends simple sports."[5]
>
> —*Time* Magazine, Asia edition

Yao's progress has been more rapid than many anticipated, and with his success came deserved respect. A month into the 2002–03 season, Dallas squelched the Rockets despite Yao's season high of 30 points, and Mavericks owner Mark Cuban still complained, "Yao was getting the calls of a 30-year veteran."[6] By their midseason report, *SI* had changed its tune and named Yao Rookie of the Year.[7]

But there were still speed bumps along the Rockets' road. In the home stretch of the 2002–03 season, Tomjanovich was diagnosed with superficial bladder cancer on March 17, 2003. Forced to undergo emergency treatment, Tomjanovich had to leave the team in the hands of assistant coach Larry Smith. Shaken by this unexpected crisis, the Rockets felt the loss of Tomjanovich, for as Yao noted, "Our coach is very special to us. He is our leader. He is our general."[8] Although absent from the bench, Rudy T. was credited with his 500th career victory as Houston defeated the Orlando Magic 114–93 at home on April 6, 2003.

But try as they might, the Rockets ran out of fuel at the finish line. As their post-season hopes faded, Yao reflected, "It felt like we were not opening a door but closing it."[9] Powered by rookie forward Amare Stoudemire, the Phoenix Suns nudged out the Rockets for the eighth and final Western

THE TAO OF YAO

Conference playoff spot. Previously Yao said of the 6'10",
240-lb Stoudemire, who jumped from a Florida high school
straight to the pros, "It seems like he's played for several years
already. If there aren't more players like Stoudemire in the
future, I think I can last."[10] After the season ended and before
the Suns were eliminated in the first round of the playoffs,
Stoudemire collected the NBA's Rookie of the Year trophy.
Though awarded the same honor by other experts from
ESPN, *Sports Illustrated,* and *The Sporting News,* Yao was gracious
as always: "Congratulations to Amare. This is just the start
of many years [of competition between us] to come."[11]

With Yao a unanimous selection for the All-Rookie Team,
the Rockets should have been encouraged by their accomplishments. Winning 50% more games than the year before,
Houston finished the season with a record of 43–39, thereby
engineering the second-best turnaround in the NBA after
the Golden State Warriors. Fittingly, Yao landed on *SI's*
cover a fourth time, as #7 of the 101 Most Influential Minorities in Sports (#1 was Robert Johnson, the chairman of Black
Entertainment Television who owns the NBA's latest expansion team the Charlotte Bobcats). As the highest-ranking
Asian on the list, Yao followed the athletes Tiger Woods
(#2), Serena Williams (#3), and Michael Jordan (#4), but
ranked ahead of Shaq (#13). What was the magazine's rea-
soning? Dollars and cents. Simply put, Yao "had the greatest economic impact of any NBA rookie since Michael
Jordan. Houston's home attendance rose 17%, and for the
first time in years the Rockets were a draw on the road. The
NBA is now aired on six Chinese TV networks."[12]

The Ming Is the Message

Which is dearer, fame or health?
Which is worth more, health or wealth?
Which is more harmful, gain or loss?
Hence, excessive love finally exacts its price.[13]

—Lao Tzu

Contrary to the predictions of Marx, religion is no longer the opiate of the masses. Sports are. Professional athletics have moved beyond simple recreation: they have become a multi-billion-dollar web of consumer entertainment, product placement, and merchandising. In the span of one year, Yao went from an altar boy to a high priest. The third time Yao graced the cover of *Sports Illustrated,* the headline blared "The Year of Yao Ming: He shoots, he smiles, he sells."[14] Rick Burton, executive director of the University of Oregon's Warsaw Sports Marketing Center, called the transformation that the public saw before its very eyes breathtaking: "Who Yao is today is 100 percent different than he was eight months ago. Yao is now an American idol.... He's Elvis."[15]

Like Michael Jordan before him, Yao was now in a position to cash in on his meteoric rise to fame. Yao revealed that on his own time, "I am on the computer quite often. I chat with my friends and play computer games. But I don't get to chat as much as I would like because of the time zone differences."[16] Therefore it was appropriate that his first noteworthy plug was for Apple computers. The advertisements on TV and billboards are a study in contrasts, as Yao stands side by side with the 2'8" actor Vern Troyer, known

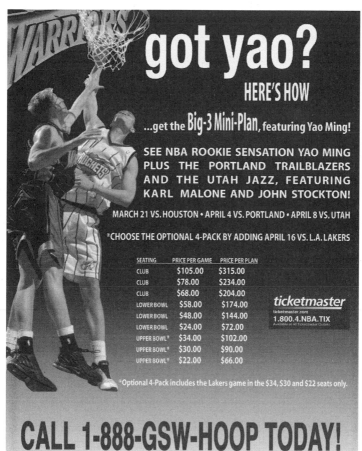

"Men in great place are thrice servants—servants of the sovereign or state, servants of fame, and servants of business."[17]

—Francis Bacon, 1625

for playing Austin Powers' movie sidekick Mini Me. When comparing laptop PowerBooks, size does matter. But in this case, Yao did think different. Analyzing the imagery a little deeper, one finds that Yao displays an underlying empathy for his tiny companion, and an earnest willingness to bridge superficial differences to find a common ground.

In that vein, Yao expressed the following: "I prefer the ads to be creative and fresh. Hopefully, the products I endorse are hi-tech and trendy."[18] Part of the marketing braintrust of "Team Yao," Bill Sanders said, "He's very technology-minded and made it clear he wants to pursue those opportunities. He won't be rushed into anything, because that's his nature. If we're patient and visionary, Yao could become a sports-marketing icon."[19]

Having thus declared his affinity for gadgets and communications, Yao signed a deal with a US startup to make a Yao Ming Basketball cell-phone game, though only 15% of China's 200 million mobile-phone users have models that can download games.[20] On the mainland, Yao signed a much bigger $4.8-million contract with telephony giant China Unicom. Tom Doctoroff, CEO of the Chinese office of J. Walter Thompson (based in Shanghai), explained the deal: "Yao Ming here is a god. He is somebody that is making it in America. The reason for hiring Yao Ming is simple: China Unicom wants to say it's a big company."[21]

Soon other endorsements followed, such as a commercial for Visa that debuted during the Super Bowl, depicting Yao having trouble shopping in a store due to a language barrier (this earned Yao his second spot on a *SI* cover and the tagline "The Real Thing"). After a full day of seventy takes, Yao explained the difference between shooting a basketball versus a commercial: "You don't get to play a game over until you get it right."[22] When asked if he a had a future as an

THE TAO OF YAO

actor, Yao listed one difficulty in his way: "I don't think they can find a stunt double for me."[23] Lastly, Yao admitted the worry that plagues all entertainers, "I just hope the people are amused by the commercials and I don't bore them."[24]

But conflict is often another sign of rising success, and soon Yao would stumble into the first controversy in his advertising career. Who would have thought he'd get embroiled in the global soda wars? Already contracted to push Pepsi's Gatorade, Yao signed another deal to endorse Pepsi Cola internationally. However, Coke had already purchased from China the license to advertise its drink using pictures from the men's national basketball team, of which Yao was still a member. Then in a textbook case of "ambush marketing," Coke unveiled ads featuring Yao, Mengke Bateer, and Guo Shiqiang in their national uniforms, right after he inked his Pepsi deal. Promptly Yao sued Coke for one yuan ($0.12) for "spiritual and economic losses" and demanded a public apology.[25]

Coca-Cola spokeswoman May Zhai defended the ads: "We insist that we have the legal right to use the images of any members of the Chinese men's basketball team on our products. According to our experience in other countries, we only need to sign the agreement with the team and there is no need for us to talk to every individual athlete to ask for their permission."[26] However, Yao faxed a statement to the Xinhua News Agency which claimed, "I have never permitted Coca-Cola to use my image to promote their products. I require Coca-Cola to withdraw all the products bearing my image and all promotion materials which use my name or images immediately."[27] It went on to say, "The only purpose of this lawsuit is to protect Yao Ming's legal rights, his rights of image and name in particular. The amount of compensation is not a focus."[28]

Even Nike was taken aback by Yao's triumphs. Certainly their initial sponsorship of Yao four years earlier had proved to be a tremendous bargain. But with a jackpot comes the taxes. Now both parties knew his services were worth much more. A Nike source said, "We don't want to hype the hell out of the guy and have him jump ship." Even before Yao was picked #1 in the NBA draft, the shoemaker tried to pre-empt the problem: it wished to "tear up" his first deal and replace it with a $1.6 million contract up to 2006. But nego-tiations broke down, and Nike could only watch as Yao's stock proceeded to go through the roof. Formerly Nike's director of marketing for China, Terry Rhoads said, "Deep in his heart, he's a Nike guy. But now it's about business."[29]

To some advertisers, Yao's biggest advantage was that he was a "blank slate." Liz Silver, Visa's senior vice president of advertising and brand management, said, "He's totally pris-tine. He hasn't had very many endorsements, or done any-thing wrong. He's just universally loved right now—except maybe by Shaq."[30] To others what he represented was very real and very right. Bill Sanders explained, "What most attracted us to Pepsi was their position as a world-class com-pany with vision and dedication, and their desire to posi-tion Yao not only as a basketball player, but as a role model and a cultural icon."[31] Now with his life firmly in the pub-lic eye, Yao was launched into an ongoing contest to control his image, focus, and life.

THE TAO OF YAO

To be favored is to be disgraced:
it is like being ensnared;
To be favored results in unseemly dependence.
It is like being ensnared if you gain it,
it is like being ensnared if you lose it.[32]

—Lao Tzu

Kareem Abdul-Jabbar was 6'8" by the time he was fourteen. But coming of age in New York, the media capital of the world, he learned to be wary of all the eyes focused upon him. As Kareem recollected,

[F]ate forced me to grow up real fast. It feels sometimes like I went straight from being a kid to where I am now, and that I have been living under the glare of public scrutiny forever. The early notoriety pushed me inside myself. Vastly outgrowing my peers physically pushed me inside too. And I was put into the position of having attention focused on me, attention mainly unwarranted, by the press, by strangers. I have always enjoyed my height—I view it as a gift—but there is a price you pay.... The world expects more from a giant, [Hall of Fame coach Joe Lapchick] told me. People scale up their demands. And since you are larger than life, you must somehow be less affected by it, as if it takes more noise to get your attention or more pain to hurt you.[33]

Just as a candle attracts moths to its flame, a celebrity magnetically draws outsiders in to catch a glimpse of stardom. Before his rookie season began, Yao poked fun at a member of the Fourth Estate: "Some reporters in China, I think their notes look like English. Yours look like Chinese."[34] At the post-game news conference after a matchup against the Warriors, Yao was asked, "What's the difference between the Chinese and American media?" Having just weathered a fusillade of inquiries from the local Chinese reporters gathered in the room from all over the San Francisco Bay Area, Yao blithely replied, "Since no American media has asked any questions yet, I don't know how to answer your question."[35] But he quickly learned that the insatiable media expects stars to be ready with quotes on demand. His rising popularity could be detrimental; Yao cautioned, "I hope the media will not start following me to the men's room."[36]

Surely they would if they could. The press incessantly seeks instant answers, pithy quotes, and nuggets of wisdom and then always seems to want more. Confronting the media throngs even at morning shootarounds before a game, Yao said on one occasion, "It's been like this since I got here. Some days I don't think there will ever be an end."[37] Primed to dissect every word, writers search for meaning between the lines. Yao was taken aback: "I have been asked so many questions, everybody knows everything."[38] Forever on the prowl, the paparazzi were cocked to capture every unflattering angle in trawling for controversy. With his private life now a matter of public record, Yao ultimately considered his hardest adjustment to be "facing the media. Those guys are hard. I thought there would be a lot of media, but I never thought there would be this many. I wouldn't say I'm sick of the media. But it does annoy me."[39]

THE TAO OF YAO

There was a price to pay for success after all. Yao realized that all those who invested something in him, whether he liked it or not, would want to exact their chunk of flesh. "Well, you have to be yourself. I try to still live my life and be myself and try not to be restricted by this cage thing fame brought with it.... For example, when I go shopping, there are a bunch of crowds surrounding me. And that makes me feel like I'm in a cage."[40]

However, Yao put on a game face and satisfied fans, press, and peers as best he could. Having done his part, he was duly recognized by the NBA and named to the "All-Interview" second team (this time Shaq was first). Recognizing a worthy opponent when he saw one, Yao professed, "After I retire from the NBA, I will probably join the mass media, because I have always been bothered by the mass media. And if I cannot beat them, I will join them."[41]

The Rise of a Shooting Star

Heaven and earth conjoin and sweet dew falls,
nobody makes this happen
but it falls equally on all.[42]

—Lao Tzu

Having seen the promised land for himself, Moses Malone concluded that the sky was the limit for Yao: "This kid can be great. He's the next in line for the Houston Rockets. I'm part of that line that ran though Dream. It means something to me. I want to see it carry on."[43] As Yao's first season progressed, ESPN's Bill Simmons revised his forecast, asking

▲ "So, we may say, stands this man, pointing as long as he lives, in obedience to some spiritual magnetism, to the summits in the historical horizon, for the guidance of his fellows."[44]

—Henry David Thoreau

rhetorically, "So what happens once he masters English, meshes with teammates and fully adjusts to the best competition in the world? He's already the second-best center in the league; with no other young rivals at his position, he has no ceiling. Forget LeBron ... the 89-inch Asian guy will

THE TAO OF YAO

dominate the NBA for the foreseeable future."[45] A former Houston Rockets guard, Frank Williams, now coach of the Phoenix Suns, agreed: "It is scary. I keep thinking, Shaq might be done in a few years and now we're going to have to deal with him."[46]

Having trod the same path before, 24-year-old Dirk Nowitzki was ensconced as one of the NBA's elite players. The first Maverick ever to be recognized as All-NBA, he led Dallas to the Western Conference Finals in the 2002–03 postseason, further than they had ever gone before. Gazing ahead, Nowitzki said Yao's future was bright indeed: "He's a great player already. He's going to keep getting better. It's amazing how he already is playing in his first year. He deserves it. He's making the game more globalized. China is watching every game now. He brought a lot to the NBA. I think he deserves all the hype.... With Yao Ming under the basket, they're going to have a great team. It's not good for us. I don't like to see Houston getting good, but they're going to be a force for probably the next decade."[47]

Inevitably, future years would pose different challenges. The first was adjusting to a new coach. On May 23, 2003, Rudy Tomjanovich tearfully resigned. In his parting press conference, he reflected on the maturation of his team: "I thought we made great strides. The competitor in me— that urge that drives me could have something to do with the disease that I have and when I wound up in the hospital with exhaustion. That part of me still wants to do that stuff, but I know that right now what is best for me is to take a lesser role. To take those burdens off of me. So that's tough because I really feel good about this team. We did make great strides."[48] Saddened at the news, Yao contemplated, "Rudy has accomplished a great deal during his years with the Rockets, and I feel fortunate to have had the time with him during my rookie season."[49]

But there was no rest for the wicked. Already Yao planned to return to China ten days after the Rockets' season ended to practice with the national team, which would play in May 2003 in the qualifying tournament for the Asian Olympics.[50] Compelled by current events, Yao proceeded to host a live three-hour TV show in Shanghai on May 11, 2003, to raise money to treat SARS. Yao said, "I just feel that there is an obligation as a celebrity to repay society and lead the way for other Chinese basketball players to do more in the way of community service. This is a great opportunity to do that and a great cause."[51]

As the death toll rose to 350 from more than 5,000 known cases, Yao said, "I returned to my motherland, but found it struggling through a most serious trial. Now everyone needs to make their contribution to the fight against SARS."[52] The telethon featured an online auction of donated sports memorabilia and videotaped messages from NBA stars like Magic Johnson and Shaq who said, "I love you, xie xie, peace," (Mandarin for thank you).[53] Broadcast to millions of viewers and sponsored by NBA, Pepsi, Gatorade, Kodak, China Unicom, among others, the program raised over $300,000, with teammate Steve Francis and Reebok both contributing $10,000.[54]

Then on June 9, 2003, Jeff Van Gundy accepted the job of coaching the Rockets. Recently a poster boy for NBA burn-out, Van Gundy now was raring to go. He explained why he jumped at the opportunity to come to Houston:

You don't get a lot of chances—I've said this before to somebody I really trust in basketball, and I asked him what he thought were the plusses and minuses. He said that the biggest plus about Houston was that every day that Yao Ming wakes up, he's 7-5. Isn't that the truth. It's very hard to fill the two positions—center and point guard—and the Rockets have done a great job getting that base. They also have Cuttino [Mobley] and a great core to build from. Those jobs—where you have a good center and point guard and a good nucleus of youth—that's hard to find.[55]

In a prepared statement Yao responded to the report of his new coach: "I felt very lucky to play for a Hall of Fame coach last year in Rudy Tomjanovich, and I feel lucky to now play for another of the best coaches in the game. I am aware of the work that Coach Van Gundy did with Patrick Ewing during the peak of his career, and I think he can bring out the best in me and all of my teammates. I believe Coach Van Gundy can help lead the Rockets to the next level."[56]

Yao's mother Fang Feng Di remarked, "There is an expression in China. Bystanders sometimes see things more clearly than the person in the middle of the situation."[57]

That was true for her baby boy, who found himself in the eye of a hurricane. Around him swirled the speculations of observers the world over who were tracking his unpredictable path and the impact left in his wake. In his dizzying whirlwind of travel, games, interviews, and reports, strangers endlessly debated his performances, preferences, and personality. Yet despite this pressure, Yao has displayed an unusual aplomb, adroitness, and awareness of his position. Conceivably, he has taken a page out of *The Book of the Way*:

> *Just remain in the center, watching, then forget that you are there.*[58]
> —Lao Tzu

Despite the vagaries of translation and interpretation, Yao has become as much a statesman as a sportsman. Plus, it always helps one's popularity to have a big funny bone. But Yao is qualitatively different from his notable and quotable predecessors. Like a Magic Johnson or Lance Armstrong, Yao has displayed both genuine enthusiasm and a mortal courage that dissolve the barriers between athlete and fan. He has done so on a global scale, shouldering the expectations and bearing the scrutiny of so many every time he touches the ball. Following his first NBA game against Indiana, which was televised to almost as many homes in China (287 million) as the total US population, Yao uttered, "I can't even comprehend the number of people who are watching me. Two hundred million people ... that means 400 million eyes."[59]

Wrapping up his first full year in America, Yao said, "I guess people did not know much about people from China."[60] Interviewing Yao for an hour-long MSNBC TV special for *National Geographic Explorer*, host Lisa Ling summarized his cultural importance: "For China, he encompasses everything that [people] want to be. He's larger than life, strong, intelligent, an international star, a family man, and a team player. He embodies much of what China is

> "When it comes to predictions, most basketball anoraks will stop at nothing.... Yao Ming, late of the Shanghai Sharks, has become a presence, and could become the most dominant player in history."[62]
>
> —*Sunday Herald,* UK

becoming."[61] But even though China has produced a series of world-class athletes, from gymnasts and divers to figure skaters, they had never seen anything quite like him. Rooted in Eastern values but open to Western influences, Yao was nicknamed "The Golden Bridge" at home for his unique potential to connect two worlds. As Yao said himself after he was drafted, "Maybe we can create a new culture together."[63]

Phil Jackson wrote, "What I've learned as a coach, and parent, is that when people are not awed or overwhelmed by authority, true authority is attained, to paraphrase the *Tao Te Ching.*"[64] Lao's actual words were:

Therefore, if one desires to be over the people,
One must speak as if under them;
If one desires to be in front of the people,
One must speak as if behind them ...
The whole world is happy to draw near him and does not
tire of him.
Because he does not compete,
Absolutely no one can compete with him.[65]

—Lao Tzu

In a world marked by cultural division and self-segregation, Yao has managed to win the acceptance of his team and league, city and host country. Initially attracting attention because of his spectacular height, he has fostered an enduring following due to his sensitivity and selflessness. Bill Walton summarized his impressions:

> When I watch Yao Ming play, I'm reminded of Magic Johnson. He makes plays like [chess champions] Garry Kasparov, like Bobby Fisher. You sit there and say, 'No way he thought of that. That had to be luck.' [Larry] Bird was that way, too—always so far ahead of everyone else mentally.... There is no limit to what he can accomplish. Yao Ming has the potential, the capability, of changing the future of basketball. [Yao] is light years ahead, minutes ahead, hours ahead of the play that's actually going on. The anticipation, the analysis, the figuring out of what's going to happen next. This is an unbelievable talent we are so lucky to have.... If you play with Yao Ming, like playing with Sabonis, like playing with Vlade Divac, you have to learn to move, learn to expect and anticipate that you'll get the ball in perfect position ... no one has ever had a more difficult period of adjustment. No one has done anything as hard as Yao Ming ... he's doing terrific. His learning curve is almost vertical.[66]

Of course, his life will constantly change as he garners more athletic achievements, commercial endorsements, and media recognition. But from avowedly humble beginnings, Yao has become not only a trailblazer in sports but a fascinating prism for society at large.

More than simply amusing, Yao's statements are instructive. Containing meaning far beyond their face value, they lead one to a deeper source of understanding of what it means to be alive. Through the words of Lao Tzu as well as those of today's famed coaches and players, Yao taps into a wellspring of wisdom, which yields insights far beyond his own experience. The modern compass can trace its ancestry to the magnetic lodestones discovered by the Chinese during the era of the Warring States, which were later refined to guide sailors who charted the stars. Created in this same period, Taoism continues to help point the way for people to live their lives today.

Though Yao may not consciously intend it, he has become an authentic teacher of Taoist values to an awestruck yet accepting world. From East to West and back again, Yao is a twenty-first-century role model not only for basketball but also for life.

Or as Yao would put it, "You can't say I've succeeded; I've just started."[67]

Appendix

Statistics

China Basketball League Regular Season (Shanghai Sharks)

Season	G	FGM	FGA	PCT	FTM	FTA	PCT	REB	AST	PTS
1997–98	21	91	148	62%	32	66	49%	175	13	210
Avg		4.3	7.0		1.5	3.1		8.3	0.6	10.0
1998–99	12	100	171	59%	51	73	70%	155	7	251
Avg		8.3	14.3		4.3	6.1		12.9	0.6	20.9
1999–00	33	285	487	59%	127	186	68%	480	57	699
Avg	–	8.6	14.8		3.8	5.6		14.5	1.7	21.2
2000–01	22	221	326	68%	139	174	80%	426	48	596
Avg		10.0	14.8		6.3	7.9		19.4	2.2	27.1
2001–02	34	411	570	72%	255	336	76%	645	98	1,102
Avg		12.1	16.8		7.5	9.9		19.0	2.9	32.4
Totals	122	1,108	1,702	65%	604	835	72%	1,881	223	2,858
Avg		9.1	14.0		5.0	6.8		15.4	1.8	23.4

2000 Olympic Games

Team	G	FGM	FGA	PCT	FTM	FTA	PCT	REB	AST	PTS
China	6	23	36	63.9%	17	24	70.6%	36	10	63
Avg		3.8	6.0		2.8	4.0		6.0	1.7	10.5

2001 Asian Championships for Men

Team	G	FGM	FGA	PCT	FTM	FTA	PCT	REB	AST	PTS
China	8	42	58	72.4%	23	24	95.8%	81	5	101
Avg		5.3	7.3		2.9	3.0		10.1	0.6	12.6

China Basketball League Playoffs (Shanghai Sharks)

Season	G	FGM	FGA	PCT	FTM	FTA	PCT	REB	AST	PTS
2001–02	10	147	192	76.6%	82	110	74.5%	202	35	389
Avg		14.7	19.2		8.2	11.0		20.2	3.5	38.9

FIBA 2002 World Championships

	Games	Minutes	FGM-A	FTM-A	Offensive	Defensive	Total Rebounds	Assists	Steals	Blocked Shots	Turn Overs	Personal Fouls	Points
Total	8	219	54-72	57-76	54	19	73	18	6	17	22	23	168
Avg		27.4	75.0%	75.0%	6.8	2.4	9.1	2.3	0.8	2.1	2.8	2.9	21.0

NBA 2002-03 Statistics
• Yao Ming started 72 out of 82 games

TEAM	G	MIN	FGM-A	FTM-A	OFF	DEF	TOT	AST	STL	BLK	TO	PF	PTS
HOU	82	2,382	401-805	301-371	196	479	675	137	31	147	173	230	1,104
Avg		29.0	49.8%	81.1%	2.4	5.8	8.2	1.7	0.4	1.8	2.1	2.8	13.5

THE TAO OF YAO

2002–03 NBA Highlights

Points:	**30** vs. Dallas (November 21, 2002)
Field Goals Made:	**10** (three times)
Field Goals Attempted:	**19** (two times)
Three-Point Field Goals Made:	**1** vs. Golden State (March 21, 2003)
Free Throws Made	**11/13** vs. Utah (February 11, 2003)
Offensive Rebounds	**8** (two times)
Defensive Rebounds	**15** vs. Sacramento (March 23, 2003)
Total Rebounds	**19** vs. Sacramento (March 23, 2003)
Assists	**6** vs. Sacramento (February 2, 2003)
Steals	**2** (five times)
Blocks	**6** (two times)

2002-03: NBA Player Rank

#15 in Field-Goal Percentage (0.498)
#14 in Defensive Rebounds (479)
#18 in Total Rebounds (675)
#18 in Rebounds Per Game (8.2)
#14 in Blocks (147)
#15 in Blocks Per Game (1.79)
#16 in Double-doubles (27)
#13 in Efficiency Ranking Per 48 Minutes (29.16)
Formula = ((Points + Rebounds + Assists + Steals + Blocks) - (Field Goals Attempted - Field Goals Made) + (Free Throws Attempted - Free Throws Made) + Turnovers)) / Games Played

Endnotes

Chapter 1. The Wonder of Yao

1. Cheng Man-Ching, Tam Gibbs (Translator), *Lao-Tzu, My Words Are Very Easy to Understand* (Berkeley, CA: North Atlantic Books, 2nd edition, April 1982), Chapter 70.

2. Margaret Mead, *Coming of Age in Samoa*, 1928.

3. *The New York Times*, February 26, 2003.

4. *NBA Inside Stuff*, May 2003, p. 48.

5. ESPN.com, December 20, 2002.

6. Bill Russell and Taylor Branch, *Second Wind: The Memoirs of an Opinionated Man* (New York: Fireside, 1979), p. 52.

7. *Los Angeles Times*, June 13, 2002, p. A1.

8. ESPN.com, September 3, 2002.

9. *ESPN The Magazine*, December 25, 2000, vol. 3, no. 26.

10. *New Jersey Star Ledger*, March 31, 2003.

11. *Miami Herald*, September 17, 2000.

12. *Saint Paul Pioneer Press*, September 17, 2000.

13. *ESPN The Magazine*, December 25, 2000, vol. 3, no. 26.

14. ESPN.com, December 13, 2000.

15. John Feinstein, *The Punch: One Night, Two Lives, and the Fight that Changed Basketball Forever* (Boston: Little, Brown, and Co., 2002), p. 325.

16. Kareem Abdul-Jabbar with Mignon McCarthy, *Kareem* (New York: Random House, 1990), p. 106; Earvin "Magic" Johnson with William Novak, *My Life* (New York: Random House, 1992), p. 179.

17. http://www.nba.com/rockets/news/Rockets_Win_2002_NBA_Draft_Lot-44865-34.html.

18. *Seattle Times*, April 26, 2002.

19. *Houston Chronicle*, August 25, 2002.

20. *Houston Chronicle*, June 28, 2002.

21. Ibid.

22. *Houston Chronicle*, May 1, 2002.

23. *The New York Times*, October 21, 2002, p. D10.

24. *Houston Chronicle,* October 21, 2002.

25. Bill Russell, *Second Wind,* p. 179.

Chapter 2. The Meaning of the Tao

1. Thomas Cleary, *The Essential Tao: An Initiation into the Heart of Tao-ism through the Authentic Tao te Ching and the Inner Teachings of Chuang Tzu* (San Francisco: HarperSanFrancisco, 1992), Chapter 62.

2. Mark Twain [Samuel Langhorne Clemens], "What Is Man?" 1906. Section 2.

3. Cheng Man-Ching, Tam Gibbs (Translator), *Lao-Tzu, My Words Are Very Easy to Understand* (Berkeley, CA: North Atlantic Books, 2nd edition, April 1982), Chapter 40.

4. Cheng Man-Ching, *Lao-Tzu, My Words Are Very Easy to Understand,* Chapter 25.

5. CNNSI.com, January 13, 2003.

6. *Houston Chronicle,* April 9, 2003.

7. Ibid.

8. *Houston Chronicle,* April 10, 2003.

9. Thomas Cleary, *The Essential Tao,* Chapter 24.

10. *Houston Chronicle,* April 13, 2003.

11. *Houston Chronicle,* February 8, 2003.

12. *San Francisco Chronicle,* November 27, 2002.

13. Press Conference after Golden State Warriors game, March 21, 2003.

14. *The New York Times,* January 18, 2003.

15. *Associated Press,* December 8, 2001.

16. *NY Daily News,* November 26, 2002.

17. *Houston Chronicle,* August 25, 2002.

18. *Boston Globe,* February 24, 2003.

19. *Tao Te Ching,* Chapter 8.

Chapter 3. The Wisdom of Lao

1. *Tao Te Ching,* Chapter 41.

2. Stephen Hodge, *The Illustrated Tao Te Ching: A New Translation*

and Commentary (Hauppauge, NY: Barron's, 2002), p. 14.

3. *ESPN The Magazine*, December 2, 2002.

4. *Houston Chronicle*, November 5, 2002.

5. Stephen Mitchell, *Tao Te Ching* (New York: Harper Collins, 1988), Chapter 27, p. viii.

6. Bill Russell and Taylor Branch, *Second Wind: The Memoirs of an Opinionated Man* (New York: Fireside, 1979), p.157.

7. Thomas Cleary, *The Essential Tao: An Initiation into the Heart of Taoism through the Authentic Tao te Ching and the Inner Teachings of Chuang Tzu* (San Francisco: HarperSanFrancisco, 1992), Chapter 33.

8. *Houston Chronicle*, October 21, 2002.

9. *San Jose Mercury News*, November 27, 2002.

10. Press Conference after Golden State Warriors game, March 21, 2003.

11. Thomas Cleary, *The Essential Tao*, Chapter 4.

12. *NBA Inside Stuff*, May 2003, p. 51.

13. Cheng Man-Ching, *Lao-Tzu, My Words Are Very Easy to Understand*, Chapter 78.

14. Ibid., Chapter 2.

15. Ibid., Chapter 63.

16. Ibid., Chapter 16.

Chapter 4. The Cultural Ambassador

1. Paul Zweig, *The Adventurer: The Fate of Adventure in the Western World* (Princeton, NJ: Princeton University Press, 1974), Chapter 3.

2. Stephen Mitchell, *Tao Te Ching* (New York: Harper Collins, 1988), Chapter 44.

3. *Associated Press*, November 15, 2002.

4. *Pioneer Press*, February 5, 2003.

5. *Houston Chronicle*, December 24, 2002.

6. Ibid.

7. Ibid

8. *Sports Illustrated for Kids*, May 2003.

9. Stephen Mitchell, *Tao Te Ching*, Chapter 24.

10. *The Sporting News*, January 20, 2003, p. 8.

11. Stephen Mitchell, *Tao Te Ching* (New York: Harper Collins, 1988), Chapter 14.

12. *USA Today*, October 28, 2002.

13. Walter Lippmann, *A Preface to Politics*, 1914. Chapter 6.

14. Lehman Brothers report, "China: Gigantic Possibilities, Present Realities," 2002.

15. *English People's Daily*, October 22, 2002.

16. *The New York Times*, January 12, 2003.

17. *Associated Press*, July 1, 2003.

18. *The New York Times*, February 9, 2003.

19. *Los Angeles Times*, June 13, 2002, p. A1.

20. *Miami Herald*, June 24, 2002.

21. *The New York Times*, January 12, 2003.

22. *Houston Chronicle*, December 24, 2002.

23. Ibid.

24. *Washington Post*, December 14, 2002.

25. *Houston Chronicle*, November 23, 2002.

26. Earvin "Magic" Johnson with William Novak, *My Life* (New York: Random House, 1992), p. 171.

27. Stephen Hodge, *The Illustrated Tao Te Ching: A New Translation and Commentary* (Hauppauge, NY: Barron's, 2002), Chapter 35.

28. *Houston Chronicle*, April 2, 2003.

29. *Newsday*, February 9, 2003.

30. *ESPN The Magazine*, February 17, 2003, p. 16.

31. *The Philadelphia Inquirer*, April 3, 2003.

32. www.nba.com/history/players/barkley_bio.html

33. *Miami Herald*, June 24, 2002.

34. *New York Daily News*, July 15, 2002.

35. *ESPN The Magazine*, February 17, 2003, p. 54.

36. ESPN.com, September 3, 2002.

37. *Houston Chronicle*, November 13, 2002.

38. *ESPN The Magazine*, December 25, 2000.

39. *Houston Chronicle*, November 13, 2002.

40. *CBS Sportsline*, November 27, 2002.

41. *San Diego Union-Tribune*, February 18, 2003.

42. WayMoreSports.com, November 2, 2002.

43. *Wall Street Journal*, Classroom Edition, December 2002.

44. *The New York Times*, December 16, 2002.

45. *The Philadelphia Inquirer*, April 3, 2003.

46. *Houston Chronicle*, April 2, 2003.

47. Ibid.

48. Ibid.

49. *Sports Illustrated*, February 10, 2003, p. 36.

50. *The Philadelphia Inquirer*, April 3, 2003.

51. *Dallas Morning News*, February 7, 2003.

52. *San Francisco Business Times*, October 11, 2002.

53. http://slam.canoe.ca/StatsBKP/BC-BKP-STAT-GOLDEN-STATTCOMP-R.html.

53. *Houston Chronicle*, October 21, 2002.

54. *The New York Times*, December 16, 2002.

55. Ibid.

56. *Associated Press*, February 9, 2003.

57. *The New York Times*, February 26, 2003.

58. *The Dallas Morning News*, January 21, 2003.

59. *The New York Times*, February 7, 2003.

60. Cheng Man-Ching, Tam Gibbs (Translator), *Lao-Tzu, My Words Are Very Easy to Understand* (Berkeley, CA: North Atlantic Books, 2nd edition, April 1982), Chapter 61.

61. *Miami Herald*, December 17, 2002.

62. *Houston Chronicle*, November 30, 2002.

63. Ron Thomas, *They Cleared the Lane: The NBA's Black Pioneers* (Lincoln, NE: University of Nebraska Press, 2002), p. 18.

64. Bill Russell and Taylor Branch, *Second Wind: The Memoirs of an Opinionated Man* (New York: Fireside, 1979), p. 187.

65. Black Athlete Sports Network, December 31, 2001.

66. *Colorlines*, Spring 2000.

67. *Miami Herald*, July 30, 2002.

68. *Los Angeles Times,* July 3, 2003, p. A1.

69. *San Francisco Chronicle,* July 2, 2003, p. A1.

70. *New York Post,* February 21, 2003.

71. *Washington Post,* February 27, 2003.

72. *Sunday Times* (London, England), September 8, 2002, p. 27.

73. *Orlando Sentinel,* January 9, 2003.

74. *Washington Post,* February 27, 2003.

75. *Associated Press,* February 9, 2003.

76. *Houston Chronicle,* December 17, 2002.

77. *USA Today,* October 28, 2002.

78. US Census, 2002, 2000, and 1990.

79. Warren I. Cohen, *The Asian American Century* (Cambridge, MA: Harvard University Press, 2002), p. 126.

80. *Wall Street Journal,* June 11, 2003, p. B5A.

81. *The Providence Journal,* February 24, 2003.

82. Morning practice at University of San Francisco, March 21, 2003.

Chapter 5. The Rookie

1. *Tao Te Ching,* Chapter 64.

2. *USA Today,* October 28, 2002.

3. ESPN.com, June 21, 2002.

4. *Miami Herald,* June 24, 2002.

5. Lewis Mumford, *The Conduct of Life* (New York: Harcourt, 1951).

6. David Halberstam, *The Breaks of the Game* (New York: Alfred E. Knopf, 1981), p. 307.

7. *Portland Tribune,* August 23, 2002.

8. *Houston Chronicle,* October 21, 2002.

9. *USA Today,* October 29, 2002.

10. Earvin "Magic" Johnson with William Novak, *My Life* (New York: Random House, 1992), p. 115.

11. *Houston Chronicle,* August 25, 2002.

12. *English People's Daily,* October 31, 2002.

13. Magic Johnson, *My Life,* p. 103.

14. http://www.yaomingmania.com/quotesfromyao.html, September 6, 2002.

15. *Houston Chronicle*, October 24, 2002.

16. Ibid.

17. *English People's Daily*, October 31, 2002.

18. Magic Johnson, *My Life*, p. 101.

19. *Houston Chronicle*, November 15, 2002.

20. *Sacramento Bee*, October 28, 2001.

21. *ESPN The Magazine*, March 5, 2001.

22. *Houston Chronicle*, December 1, 2002.

23. Ibid.

24. *Milwaukee Journal Sentinel*, February 8, 2003.

25. NBA conference call, January 31, 2003.

26. *San Francisco Examiner*, November 28, 2002.

27. *The New York Times*, January 18, 2003.

28. *Detroit Free Press*, February 7, 2003.

29. *The New York Times*, February 7, 2003.

30. Stephen Mitchell, *Tao Te Ching* (New York: Harper Collins, 1988), Chapter 8.

31. *CBS Sportsline*, November 5, 2002.

32. ESPN.com, August 7, 2002.

33. *Christian Science Monitor*, April 23, 2002.

34. *Milwaukee Journal Sentinel*, July 31, 2002.

35. *Saint Paul Pioneer Press*, September 17, 2000.

36. TNT, "Inside the NBA," November 14, 2002.

37. *Associated Press*, November 15, 2002.

38. *Houston Chronicle*, November 22, 2002.

39. *Houston Chronicle*, November 19, 2002.

40. *Houston Chronicle*, November 23, 2002.

41. *Associated Press*, November 21, 2002.

42. *Houston Chronicle*, November 23, 2002.

43. Ibid.

44. http://sportsillustrated.cnn.com/basketball/news/2003/01/13/talking_trash/

45. *Houston Chronicle,* November 23, 2002.

46. Ibid.

47. *Houston Chronicle,* February 1, 2003.

48. ESPN.com, December 18, 2002.

49. ESPN.com, December 20, 2002.

50. *San Francisco Examiner,* December 4, 2002.

51. ESPN.com, November 23, 2002.

52. *Tao Te Ching,* Chapter 71.

Chapter 6. The Art of Traveling

1. *Tao Te Ching,* Chapter 64.

2. *Miami Herald,* September 3, 2002.

3. Ibid.

4. *Philadelphia Daily News,* April 4, 2003.

5. *ESPN The Magazine,* December 25, 2000.

6. Henry David Thoreau, *The Writings of Henry David Thoreau* (Boston: Houghton Mifflin, 1906), Vol. 4, p. 41.

7. *Houston Chronicle,* October 24, 2002.

8. *Houston Chronicle,* January 11, 2003.

9. *The New York Times,* June 30, 2002 and *San Francisco Chronicle,* November 28, 2002.

10. NBA.com, December 10, 2002.

11. Stephen Mitchell, *Tao Te Ching* (New York: Harper Collins, 1988), Chapter 27.

12. Kareem Abdul-Jabbar with Mignon McCarthy, *Kareem* (New York: Random House, 1990), p. 105.

13. *Seattle Times,* November 30, 2002.

14. *The New York Times,* February 7, 2003.

15. *USA Today,* October 29, 2002.

16. *New York Post,* February 25, 2003.

17. *Houston Chronicle,* November 30, 2002.

18. NBA.com, December 10, 2002.

19. *Houston Chronicle,* January 28, 2003.

20. *Slam magazine,* May 2003, p. 102.

21. Cheng Man-Ching, Tam Gibbs (Translator), *Lao-Tzu, My Words Are Very Easy to Understand* (Berkeley, CA: North Atlantic Books, 2nd edition, April 1982), Chapter 47.

22. *Houston Chronicle*, February 8, 2003.

23. *San Francisco Examiner*, November 27, 2002.

24. Bill Walton with Gene Wojciechowski, *Nothing but Net: Just Give Me the Ball and Get out of the Way* (New York: Hyperion, 1994), p.17.

25. Earvin "Magic" Johnson with William Novak, *My Life* (New York: Random House, 1992), p. 103.

26. Kareem Abdul-Jabbar, *Kareem*, p. 105.

27. *ESPN The Magazine*, February 17, 2003.

28. Cheng Man-Ching, Tam Gibbs (Translator), *Lao-Tzu, My Words Are Very Easy to Understand* (Berkeley, CA: North Atlantic Books, 2nd edition, April 1982), Chapter 22.

29. *Houston Chronicle*, March 26, 2003.

30. Cheng Man-Ching, *Lao-Tzu, My Words Are Very Easy to Understand*, Chapter 67.

31. NBA.com, December 10, 2002.

32. *Newsday*, February 9, 2003.

33. John Feinstein, *The Punch: One Night, Two Lives, and the Fight that Changed Basketball Forever* (Boston: Little, Brown, and Co., 2002), p. 324.

34. *Houston Chronicle*, December 24, 2002.

35. *Detroit Free Press*, February 7, 2003.

36. *The New York Times*, February 26, 2003.

37. John Feinstein. *The Punch*, p. 171.

38. *Slam magazine*, May, 2003, p. 104.

39. *Christian Science Monitor*, April 23, 2002.

40. Knight Ridder/Tribune News Service, June 30, 2002, *Milwaukee Journal Sentinel*.

41. *Slam magazine*, May 2003, p. 100.

42. *Oakland Tribune*, November 27, 2002.

43. NBA.com, December 10, 2002.

44. *Houston Chronicle*, December 24, 2002.

45. Ibid.

46. ESPN.com, September 3, 2002.

47. *Houston Chronicle*, November 28, 2002.

48. *Houston Chronicle*, November 15, 2002.

49. *Houston Chronicle*, November 28, 2002.

50. NBA.com, December 10, 2002.

51. *English People's Daily*, February 6, 2002.

52. *Press of Atlantic City*, April 4, 2003.

53. Stephen Mitchell, *Tao Te Ching*, Chapter 26.

54. *ESPN The Magazine*, February 17, 2003, p. 47.

55. *The Sporting News*, January 20, 2003, p. 8.

56. NBA.com, December 10, 2002.

57. *USA Today*, October 29, 2002.

58. *Washington Post*, February 28, 2003, p. D1.

59. ESPN.com, December 18, 2002.

60. *Associated Press*, February 9, 2003.

61. http://www.houstonareasurvey.org.

62. ESPN.com, September 3, 2002.

63. *Washington Post*, February 27, 2003, p. D4.

64. *Associated Press*, November 13, 2002.

65. *Houston Chronicle*, December 24, 2002.

66. *Houston Chronicle*, November 1, 2002.

67. *Associated Press*, November 15, 2002.

68. *Houston Chronicle*, November 28, 2002.

69. Morning practice at University of San Francisco, March 21, 2003.

70. *Press of Atlantic City*, April 4, 2003.

71. *Houston Chronicle*, November 1, 2002.

72. Rockets.com, April 7, 2003.

73. ESPN.com, December 24, 2002.

Chapter 7. The Aim of Athletics

1. *Houston Chronicle*, December 4, 2002.

2. *Tao Te Ching*, Chapter 7.

3. Bob Mitchell, *The Tao of Sports* (Berkeley, CA: North Atlantic Books, 1997).

4. Ibid., p. xi.

5. Germaine Greer, *The Change: Women, Aging and the Menopause* (New York: Ballantine Books, 1991), Chapter 2.

6. Bill Russell and Taylor Branch, *Second Wind: The Memoirs of an Opinionated Man* (New York: Fireside, 1979), p.157.

7. John Wooden with Jack Tobin, *They Call Me Coach* (Chicago: Contemporary Books, 1988) p. 169.

8. *Encyclopedia Britannica* ("Olympic Games" entry).

9. Bill Russell, *Second Wind*, p. 188.

10. Cheng Man-Ching, Tam Gibbs (Translator), *Lao-Tzu, My Words Are Very Easy to Understand* (Berkeley, CA: North Atlantic Books, 2nd edition, April 1982), Chapter 56.

11. *Houston Chronicle*, August 25, 2002.

12. *Houston Chronicle*, December 20, 2002.

13. *Sunday Times* (London, England), September 8, 2002, p. 27.

14. *Sports Illustrated*, January 27, 2003.

15. *Houston Chronicle*, December 20, 2002.

16. *Associated Press*, March 31, 2003.

17. Stephen Hodge, *The Illustrated Tao Te Ching: A New Translation and Commentary* (Hauppauge, NY: Barron's, 2002), Chapter 68.

18. *USA Today*, December 9, 2002.

19. *Taipei Times*, January 19, 2003.

20. John Feinstein, *The Punch: One Night, Two Lives, and the Fight that Changed Basketball Forever* (Boston: Little, Brown, and Co., 2002), p. 253.

21. *Associated Press*, November 15, 2002.

22. *English People's Daily*, October 31, 2002.

23. *The New York Times*, February 26, 2003.

24. *Houston Chronicle*, November 22, 2002.

25. Kareem Abdul-Jabbar with Mignon McCarthy, *Kareem* (New York: Random House, 1990), p. 5.

26. *Toronto Star*, March 6, 2003.

27. *Los Angeles Times*, March 2, 2003 p. D 6.

28. *San Francisco Examiner*, November 28, 2002.

29. Thomas Cleary, *The Essential Tao: An Initiation into the Heart of Taoism through the Authentic Tao te Ching and the Inner Teachings of Chuang Tzu* (San Francisco: HarperSanFrancisco, 1992), Chapter 39.

30. *ESPN The Magazine*, February 17, 2003, p. 44.

31. *San Diego Union-Tribune*, February 18, 2003.

32. ESPN.com, September 3, 2002.

33. Ibid.

34. *Associated Press*, December 30, 2002.

35. *English People's Daily*, January 6, 2003.

36. *The Sporting News*, January 17, 2003.

37. *Tao Te Ching*, Chapter 17.

38. *Houston Chronicle*, October 26, 2002.

39. ESPN.com, September 3, 2002.

40. *Houston Chronicle*, October 26, 2002.

41. *The New York Times*, February 7, 2003.

42. *Washington Post*, January 29, 2003, p. D1.

43. *Houston Chronicle*, October 26, 2002.

44. Ibid.

45. *Houston Chronicle*, November 3, 2002.

46. *Houston Chronicle*, February 8, 2003.

47. *The New York Times*, February 7, 2003.

48. John Feinstein, *The Punch*, p. 174.

49. Ibid., p. 175.

50. *The New York Times*, February 7, 2003.

51. CNNSI.com, January 8, 2003.

52. http://www.yaomingmania.com/quotes.html, December 10, 2002.

53. http://global.nba.com/rockets/news/RocketsPacers_Postgame_Quotes-56934-34.html, October 30, 2002.

54. *Houston Chronicle*, December 28, 2002.

55. *New York Daily News*, July 15, 2002.

56. *Miami Herald*, June 24, 2002.

THE TAO OF YAO

57. *New York Daily News*, July 15, 2002.

58. Sportsillustrated.cnn.com, January 13, 2003.

59. Stephen Hodge, *The Illustrated Tao Te Ching*, Chapter 27.

60. *NBA Inside Stuff*, May 2003, p. 48.

61. John Wooden, *They Call Me Coach*, p. 168.

62. Kareem Abdul-Jabbar, *Kareem*, p. 91.

63. Bill Walton with Gene Wojciechowski, *Nothing but Net: Just Give Me the Ball and Get out of the Way* (New York: Hyperion, 1994), p. 66.

64. Ibid., p. 17.

65. *NBA Inside Stuff*, May 2003, p. 48.

66. SportsReporter.com

67. Bruce Jenkins, *A Good Man* (Berkeley, CA: Frog, Ltd., 1999), p. 223.

68. David Halberstam, *The Breaks of the Game* (New York: Alfred E. Knopf, 1981), p. 209.

69. Bruce Jenkins, *A Good Man*, p. 264.

70. Ibid., p. 263.

71. *Houston Chronicle*, November 3, 2002.

72. John Feinstein, *The Punch*, p. 190.

73. *Christian Science Monitor*, January 17, 2003.

74. ESPN.com, January 29, 2002.

75. *Minneapolis Star Tribune*, December 21, 2002.

76. *Tao Te Ching*, Chapter 81.

77. http://www.yaomingmania.com/quotesfromyao.html, December 10, 2002.

78. John Feinstein, *The Punch*, p. 165.

79. ESPN.com, January 29, 2002.

80. *Houston Chronicle*, February 1, 2003.

81. http://www.usabasketball.com/seniormen/archive/02-mwc-exhgame1_quotes.html.

82. http://www.yaomingmania.com/quotesfromyao.html.

83. *Houston Chronicle*, February 10, 2003.

84. *ESPN The Magazine*, January 6, 2003.

85. NBA.com, http://test2.nba.com/rockets/news/What_Theyre_

Saying_About_Yao-61429-34.html.

86. *Houston Chronicle*, December 6, 2002.

87. *Houston Chronicle*, December 4, 2002.

88. *Houston Chronicle*, January 9, 2003.

89. *Houston Chronicle*, December 17, 2003.

90. *The New York Times*, December 16, 2002.

91. *Houston Chronicle*, January 3, 2003.

Chapter 8. Sports Are War

1. Stephen Hodge, *The Illustrated Tao Te Ching: A New Translation and Commentary* (Hauppauge, NY: Barron's, 2002), Chapter 69.

2. Sun Tzu/Steve Kaufman, *The Art of War* (Boston: Charles E. Tuttle, 1996), Book 1, p. 3.

3. *English People's Daily*, October 6, 2002.

4. John Leonard, *The New York Times*, November 2, 1975.

5. Pat Riley, *The Winner Within: A Life Plan for Team Players* (New York: Berkley Publishing Group, 1994), p. 104.

6. Bill Russell and Taylor Branch, *Second Wind: The Memoirs of an Opinionated Man* (New York: Fireside, 1979), p. 98.

7. Hakeem Olajuwon with Peter Knobler, *Living the Dream: My Life and Basketball* (Boston: Little, Brown and Company, 1996).

8. *New York Times*, October 2, 2003.

9. Phil Jackson with Hugh Delehanty, *Sacred Hoops: Spiritual Lessons of a Hardwood Warrior* (New York: Hyperion, 1995), p. 110.

10. *English People's Daily*, October 31, 2002.

11. *Houston Chronicle*, December 21, 2002.

12. Sun Tzu/Steve Kaufman, *The Art of War*, Book 3, p. 27.

13. Thomas Cleary, *The Essential Tao: An Initiation into the Heart of Taoism through the Authentic Tao te Ching and the Inner Teachings of Chuang Tzu* (San Francisco: HarperSanFrancisco, 1992), Chapter 33.

14. Sun Tzu/Steve Kaufman, *The Art of War*, Book 4, p. 35.

15. Pat Riley, *The Winner Within*, p. 104.

16. *Christian Science Monitor*, April 23, 2002.

17. *Associated Press*, October 21, 2002.

18. *Houston Chronicle*, November 15, 2002.

19. Pat Riley, *The Winner Within*, p. 268.

20. *Houston Chronicle*, February 10, 2003.

21. *Houston Chronicle*, December 19, 2002.

22. Clutchcity.net, January 10, 2003.

23. *ESPN The Magazine*, December 25, 2000.

24. *CBS Sportsline*, December 3, 2002.

25. Stephen Mitchell, *Tao Te Ching* (New York: Harper Collins, 1988), Chapter 30.

26. Sun Tzu/Steve Kaufman, *The Art of War*, Book 4, p. 37.

27. Kareem Abdul-Jabbar, *Kareem*, p. 204.

28. *The New York Times*, April 23, 2000.

29. Morning practice at University of San Francisco, March 21, 2003.

30. Phil Jackson, *Sacred Hoops*, p. 87.

31. Cheng Man-Ching, Tam Gibbs (Translator), *Lao-Tzu, My Words Are Very Easy to Understand* (Berkeley, CA: North Atlantic Books, 2nd edition, April 1982), Chapter 69.

32. Sun Tzu/Steve Kaufman, *The Art of War*, Book 4, p. 36.

33. Phil Jackson, *Sacred Hoops*, p. 136.

34. *Houston Chronicle*, February 3, 2003.

35. *English People's Daily*, October 31, 2002.

36. *Houston Chronicle*, November 21, 2002.

37. *Houston Chronicle*, December 6, 2002.

38. NBA post-game comments, December 21, 2002.

39. *Houston Chronicle*, December 28, 2002.

40. *Houston Chronicle*, December 20, 2002.

41. Sun Tzu/Steve Kaufman, *The Art of War*, Book 1, p. 7.

42. www.yaomingmania.com/quotes.html, December 2002.

43. *Philadelphia Daily News*, April 4, 2003.

44. ESPN.com, September 3, 2002.

45. Cheng Man-Ching, *Lao-Tzu, My Words Are Very Easy to Understand*, Chapter 78.

46. Sun Tzu/Steve Kaufman, *The Art of War*, Book 9, p. 75.

47. *Houston Chronicle*, June 28, 2002.

48. *Houston Chronicle*, October 21, 2002.

49. José Klein, Salon.com, May 29, 2001.

50. *Los Angeles Times*, November 18, 2002, p. D1.

51. *Houston Chronicle*, November 18, 2002.

52. Sun Tzu/Steve Kaufman, *The Art of War*, Book 1, p. 10.

53. *AsianWeek*, January 3, 2003.

54. Ibid.

55. *AsianWeek*, January 2, 2003.

56. *Houston Chronicle*, January 11, 2003.

57. Ibid.

58. *Associated Press*, January 10, 2003.

59. Sun Tzu/Steve Kaufman, *The Art of War*, Book 6, p. 50.

60. *Associated Press*, January 10, 2003.

61. Ibid.

62. *Los Angeles Times*, January 11, 2003, p. D1.

63. *Associated Press*, January 13, 2003.

64. Bill Walton with Gene Wojciechowski, *Nothing but Net: Just Give Me the Ball and Get out of the Way* (New York: Hyperion, 1994), p. 217.

65. ESPN.com, January 16, 2003.

66. *Houston Chronicle*, January 17, 2003.

67. *The New York Times*, January 18, 2003.

68. Thomas Cleary, *The Essential Tao*, Chapter 69

69. Sun Tzu/Steve Kaufman, *The Art of War*, Book 8, p. 70.

70. *Orange County Register*, January 16, 2003.

71. Ibid.

72. *Arizona Republic*, January 16, 2003.

73. *Associated Press*, January 16, 2003.

74. Ibid.

75. Stephen Hodge, *The Illustrated Tao Te Ching*, Chapter 67.

76. Sun Tzu/Steve Kaufman, *The Art of War*, Book 1, p. 9.

77. *AsianWeek*, January 24, 2003.

78. *Houston Chronicle*, November 17, 2002.

79. *ESPN The Magazine*, February 17, 2003, p. 48.

80. Sports Ticker, January 18, 2003.

81. *San Gabriel Valley Tribune*, January 18, 2003.

82. *ESPN The Magazine*, February 17, 2003, p. 48.

83. Sports Ticker, January 18, 2003.

84. *Associated Press*, January 18, 2003.

85. *San Gabriel Valley Tribune*, January 18, 2003.

86. *The New York Times*, January 18, 2003.

87. *Associated Press*, January 18, 2003.

88. *Media Life Magazine*, January 23, 2003.

89. *Los Angeles Times*, January 22, 2003, p. D5.

90. *Tao Te Ching*, Chapter 73.

91. Sun Tzu/Steve Kaufman, *The Art of War*, Book 1, p. 8.

92. *AsianWeek*, January 2, 2003.

93. *Houston Chronicle*, December 20, 2002.

94. *Associated Press*, January 12, 2003.

95. *The New York Times*, January 12, 2003.

96. *The Sporting News*, January 20, 2003, p. 10.

97. *Houston Chronicle*, January 3, 2003.

98. *Houston Chronicle*, January 24, 2003.

99. *Orange County Register*, January 30, 2003.

100. *Dallas-Ft. Worth Star Telegram*, February 16, 2003.

101. NBA conference call, January 31, 2003.

102. Ibid.

103. *The New York Times*, February 7, 2003.

104. www.yaomingmania.com, February 7, 2003.

105. *Houston Chronicle*, February 10, 2003.

106. *The Orange County Register*, March 26, 2003.

107. Cheng Man-Ching, *Lao-Tzu, My Words Are Very Easy to Understand*, Chapter 30.

108. Sun Tzu/Steve Kaufman, *The Art of War*, Book 9, p. 75.

109. Morning practice at University of San Francisco, March 21, 2003.

110. Bill Russell, *Second Wind*, p. 158.

111. Cheng Man-Ching, *Lao-Tzu, My Words Are Very Easy to Understand*, Chapter 43.

112. Stephen Mitchell, *Tao Te Ching*, p. viii.

Chapter 9. Being in the Center

1. Stephen Mitchell, *Tao Te Ching* (New York: Harper Collins, 1988), Chapter 11.

2. *English People's Daily*, October 31, 2002.

3. Alistair Cooke, "On Dag Hammarskjöld," *New York Herald Tribune*, October 4, 1957.

4. *Houston Chronicle*, February 10, 2003.

5. *The Christian Science Monitor*, April 26, 2002 p. 12.

6. *Houston Chronicle*, December 28, 2002.

7. *USA Today*, February 27, 2003.

8. *Houston Chronicle*, December 28, 2002.

9. *Los Angeles Times*, March 26, 2003 p. D-7.

10. *The Christian Science Monitor*, Jan 17, 2003.

11. *The New York Times*, February 22, 2002.

12. *The Christian Science Monitor*, April 26, 2002 p. 12.

13. *USA Today*, February 4, 2003.

14. *Houston Chronicle*, November 25, 2002.

15. http://www.yaomingmania.com/quotes.html, January 8, 2003.

16. ESPN Classic's SportsCentury TV series.

17. Bruce Jenkins, *A Good Man* (Berkeley, CA: Frog, Ltd., 1999), p. 268.

18. *Houston Chronicle*, December 28, 2002.

19. Stephen Mitchell, *Tao Te Ching*, Chapter 13.

20. *Time* Magazine, August 5, 2002, p. 68.

21. *Houston Chronicle*, April 3, 2003.

22. *Time* Magazine, Asia edition, November 18, 2002.

23. *Houston Chronicle*, August 23, 2002.

24. *Washington Post*, October 13, 1999.

25. *Associated Press*, November 21, 2002.

26. *Minneapolis Star Tribune*, December 21, 2002.

27. http://www.yaomingmania.com/quotes.html, January 7, 2003.

28. Kareem Abdul-Jabbar with Mignon McCarthy, *Kareem* (New York: Random House, 1990), p. 170.

29. *Houston Chronicle,* December 2, 2002.

30. *Sports Illustrated for Kids,* May 2003.

31. *ESPN The Magazine,* January 6, 2003.

32. *Sports Illustrated for Kids,* May 2003.

33. *Associated Press,* December 18, 2002.

34. *Associated Press,* November 10, 2002.

35. *NBA Inside Stuff,* May 2003, p. 50.

36. http://test2.nba.com/rockets/news/What_Theyre_Saying_About_Yao-61429-34.html.

37. *Sports Illustrated for Kids,* May 2003.

38. *Associated Press,* June 18. 2003.

39. *Houston Chronicle,* April 7, 2003.

40. *Houston Chronicle,* March 7, 2003.

41. Press Conference after Golden State Warriors game, March 21, 2002.

42. Stephen Mitchell, *Tao Te Ching,* Chapter 29.

Chapter 10. Lighting the Way

1. Elias Canetti, "1975," *The Secret Heart of the Clock: Notes, Aphorisms, Fragments 1973–1985* (New York: Farrar Straus & Giroux, 1989).

2. Stephen Mitchell, *Tao Te Ching* (New York: Harper Collins, 1988), Chapter 23.

3. *English People's Daily,* October 31, 2002.

4. *Sports Illustrated,* October 26, 2002, p. 70.

5. *Time* Magazine, Asia edition, April 28, 2003.

6. *Houston Chronicle,* November 22, 2002.

7. *Sports Illustrated,* February 10, 2003.

8. Morning practice at University of San Francisco, March 21, 2003.

9. *Houston Chronicle,* April 5, 2003.

10. *Los Angeles Times,* March 2, 2003, p. D6.

11. *Houston Chronicle*, April 24, 2003.

12. *Sports Illustrated*, May 5, 2003.

13. Cheng Man-Ching, Tam Gibbs (Translator), *Lao-Tzu, My Words Are Very Easy to Understand* (Berkeley, CA: North Atlantic Books, 2nd edition, April 1982), Chapter 44.

14. *Sports Illustrated*, February 10, 2003.

15. *Los Angeles Times*, April 22, 2003.

16. NBA.com, December 10, 2002.

17. Francis Bacon, *Of Great Place*, 1625.

18. NBA conference call, January 31, 2003.

19. *Sports Illustrated*, February 10, 2003, p. 37.

20. *San Francisco Chronicle*, January 25, 2003.

21. *Newsday*, February 9, 2003.

22. Ibid.

23. *Associated Press*, January 13, 2003.

24. *Pioneer Press*, February 5, 2003.

25. *Associated Press*, May 26, 2003.

26. *Reuters*, May 27, 2003.

27. ESPN.com, May 15, 2003.

28. *Houston Chronicle*, May 26, 2003.

29. *Los Angeles Times*, April 22, 2003.

30. *Reuters*, February 2, 2003.

31. ESPN.com, May 15, 2003.

32. Stephen Hodge, *The Illustrated Tao Te Ching: A New Translation and Commentary* (Hauppauge, NY: Barron's, 2002), Chapter 13.

33. Kareem Abdul-Jabbar with Mignon McCarthy, *Kareem* (New York: Random House, 1990), p. 17.

34. *Houston Chronicle*, August 25, 2002.

35. Press Conference after Golden State Warriors game, March 21, 2002.

36. *Newsday*, February 9, 2003.

37. *ESPN The Magazine*, February 17, 2003, p. 48.

38. *Sports Illustrated for Kids*, May 2003.

39. Ibid.

40. ESPN.com, September 3, 2002.

41. *The New York Times*, February 7, 2003.

42. Stephen Hodge, *The Illustrated Tao Te Ching*, Chapter 32.

43. *Houston Chronicle*, February 10, 2003.

44. Henry David Thoreau, "Thomas Carlyle and His Works," *The Writings of Henry David Thoreau* (Boston: Houghton Mifflin, 1906), vol. 4, pp. 354–355.

45. *ESPN The Magazine*, January 6, 2003.

46. *The New York Times*, December 16, 2002.

47. *Houston Chronicle*, February 8, 2003.

48. http://www.nba.com/rockets/news/Rudy_T_Steps_Down-76227-34.html.

49. *Associated Press*, May 28, 2003.

50. *Houston Chronicle*, April 10, 2003.

51. *Houston Chronicle*, May 7, 2003.

52. *Associated Press*, May 11, 2003.

53. Ibid.

54. *Canadian Press*, May 8, 2003.

55. http://www.nba.com/rockets/news/Jeff_Van_Gundy_Visits_Houston-77376-34.html.

56. *Associated Press*, June 11, 2003.

57. *Houston Chronicle*, December 24, 2002.

58. *Tao Te Ching*, Chapter 19.

59. *NBA Inside Stuff*, April 2003, p. 28.

60. *Houston Chronicle*, April 19, 2003.

61. *National Geographic News*, May 30, 2003.

62. *Sunday Herald*, UK, November 24, 2002.

63. *Houston Chronicle*, August 16, 2002.

64. Phil Jackson with Hugh Delehanty, *Sacred Hoops: Spiritual Lessons of a Hardwood Warrior* (New York: Hyperion, 1995), p. 152.

65. Cheng Man-Ching, *Lao-Tzu, My Words Are Very Easy to Understand*, Chapter 66.

66. *Houston Chronicle*, December 18, 2002.

67. *The New York Times*, December 16, 2002.

Index

A

Abdul-Jabbar, Kareem, 5, 10, 13,
72, 76, 96, 99, 119, 122,
130, 133, 154, 176,
184–187, 190, 205
skyhook, 190, 192
Acquired Immune Deficiency
Syndrome (AIDS), 39, 122,
172
acupuncture, 154–155
Adelman, Rick, 24, 98, 132, 134
adoption, 64–65
advertising, 4, 44, 52–54, 59, 95,
160, 200–204
Advertising Age, 52
Africa, 46, 169, 175
African Americans, 57–58,
69–70, 160, 197
Alexander, Les, 53
America, *see US*
American Basketball Association
(ABA), 89, 144
American Broadcasting Company
(ABC), 173
American Dream, 38, 55, 57,
60–64
Amnesty International, 39
Angola, 82
Anna, Santa, 109
Anthony, Greg, 60
AOL Time Warner, 82
Apple Computer, 200
Armstrong, Lance, 212
Asaka, Daniel, 65

Ashe, Arthur, 122
Asian Americans, 36, 59, 65,
171–172
identity, 17, 60–66, 213
politicians, 65
population, 52, 63–65, 109
Asian Games, 2002, 43, 73
Asian Olympics, 210
AsianWeek, 165, 171
Atlanta Hawks, 153
Auburn University, 80
Australia, 5–6, 115

B

Bacon, Francis, 201
Barkley, Charles, 10, 80–86, 88,
119, 126, 184, 197
Barry, Rick, 89, 138
baseball, 16, 57, 117, 121
Negro leagues, 57
basketball, 17, 47, 69–70, 100,
122, 124, 126, 137, 156
dunking, 48, 82, 93–94, 132,
153, 170, 190
fundamentals, 132–140, 145
hardship, 76, 131, 182, 189
trash talking, 118–119
Batman and Robin, 128
Baylor, Elgin, 126
Bellamy, Walt, 182
Berger, Cary, 65
Berkeley, University of California
at, 135, 137
Berra, Yogi, 16

Bird, Larry, 6, 51, 72, 75, 80, 82, 139, 167, 185, 214
Black, Joe, 57
Black Entertainment Television (BET), 199
Bobcock, Rob, 131
Bol, Manute, 4, 46
Boston Celtics, 6, 65, 116, 130, 139, 148
  Boston Garden, 118, 148
  Fleet Center, 65
Boxer Rebellion, 37
boxing, 57
Bradley, Bill, 155
Bradley, Shawn, 83, 189
Britain, 40
Brown, Dale, 167
Brown, Jim, 58, 113
Brown, Kwame, 186
Brown, Larry, 8, 138, 144
Brown, Lee, 108
Bruno, Tony, 164
Bryant, Kobe, 13, 48–49, 76, 156, 159–160, 168, 170, 183
Buckwalter, Bucky, 69–71
Buddhism, 39
  Zen, 161, 163, 190
Burton, Rick, 200
Bush, George, 108

C
California, 1849 Gold Rush, 62
Campanella, Roy, 57
Canada, 39, 188
Candy, John, 97
Canetti, Elias, 196
capitalism, 40

Chamberlain, Wilt, 113, 152, 178, 182, 189, 192
Chan, Jackie, 17
Chandler, Tyson, 186
Chang, Michael, 61
Chao, Elaine, 65
Charlotte Hornets, 76
Cheong, Sau Ching, 46
chi, 154–155, 187
Chiang, Kai-shek, 151
Chicago, 14, 107
Chicago Bears, 125
Chicago Bulls, 44, 155, 172
China, 2, 11, 27, 35–37, 39–45, 55, 91, 102, 165, 169, 173–175, 187, 202, 210, 212–213
  agriculture, 40, 105
  basketball, 8, 35, 52, 54, 73, 89, 97, 101, 103, 133, 144, 152, 173–175, 183, 188, 197, 203
  censorship, 41, 43
  conflict with US, 37
  dynasties, 27, 151
  economy, 39–42
  food, 55, 88, 104–106, 109, 175
  human rights, 39–41
  Middle Kingdom, 37
  population, 35, 41, 64–65, 174, 212
  sports, 5, 12, 42–44, 73, 133, 152
  urbanization, 41
China Central Television (CCTV), 52

THE TAO OF YAO

China Unicom, 202, 210
Chinese language, 52, 60, 164–165, 167
    Mandarin, 22–23, 53, 210
Chinese Americans, 55, 60–65
    1882 Chinese Exclusion Act, 62
    1965 Immigration and Naturalization Act, 63
Chinese Basketball Association (CBA), 4, 12, 15, 73–74, 124
    Bayi Rockets, 47
Chou, En Lai, 11
Chou Dynasty, 27
Christmas, 98, 106–107
Citadel, The, 72
Clemente, Roberto, 121
Clemons, Roger, 117
Cleveland Browns, 58
Cleveland Cavaliers, 0, 4
Clifton, Nat "Sweetwater," 58
CNN, 83, 85
Cobb, Ty, 117
Coca Cola, 203
Cohen, Warren, 64
Cold War, 11, 37
Communism, 39–40
compass, 215
Confucius, 27
Conroy, Pat, 72
Continental Basketball Association (CBA), 140
Cooke, Alistair, 181
Cooper, Chuck, 58
Cowens, Dave, 182
Cuban, Mark, 198

Cultural Revolution, 37, 103
Curry, Eddie, 186

D
Dallas Mavericks, 43, 47, 49, 74, 85, 122, 183–184, 198, 209
Daniels, Mel, 69
Daugherty, Brad, 88
Davis, Ernie, 58,
Dawson, Carroll, 107
de Coubertin, Pierre, 116
DeBusschere, Dave, 155
Deng, Xiao Ping, 40
Denver Nuggets, 7, 74, 138
Detroit Pistons, 8, 48, 71, 119
Didrikson Zacharias, Mildred "Babe," 57
DiMaggio, Joe, 113
Divac, Vlade, 47, 76–78, 132, 143, 186, 214
Doctoroff, Tom, 202
Downing, Pamela, 65
Drexler, Clyde, 10, 192
driving, 93–94, 112
Duncan, Tim, 74

E
Erving, Julius "Doctor J," 80, 184
ESPN, 3, 6, 60, 106, 123, 143, 172, 184, 192, 199, 207
Ewing, Patrick, 130, 148, 174, 182, 184, 193, 211

F
Fairleigh Dickinson University, 61
Falun Gong, 39

Fang, Feng Di, 36, 103–104, 112, 170, 211

Faulkner, Shannon, 72

Feinstein, John, 128

FIBA, 125
  2002 World Championships, 73, 86, 91, 119, 129, 142–143, 188

Films, *Austin Powers*, 201

Films, *Groundhog Day*, 96

Films, *Harry Potter*, 97

Films, *Planes, Trains, and Automobiles*, 96

Films, *Star Wars*, 154

Films, *Steel*, 160

Films, *The Lords of Discipline*, 72

Films, *Wall Street*, 149

Fisher, Bobby, 214

Fitch, Bill, 186,

football, 16, 57, 117, 157
  Super Bowl, 202,

fortune cookie, 29, 55

Fox Sports, 164–165

Francis, Steve, 28, 97, 99, 125–128, 140, 144, 153, 170, 176, 184, 194, 210–211

Frazier, Walt, 155

G

Garnett, Kevin, 83, 140, 176

Gasol, Paul, 51

Gastineau, Mark, 117

Gekko, Gordon, 149–150

Georgetown University, 130

Germany, 78, 129, 175, 197

Ginobili, Emanuel, 51

Godzilla, 59, 161

Goldberg, Michael, 16, 107

Golden State Warriors, 34, 38, 47, 52–53, 56, 89, 95, 138, 144, 194, 199, 201, 206, 208

golf, 16, 57, 59, 197

Gorbachev, Mikhail, 70

Greece, 132

Greenspan, Bud, 117

Greer, Germaine, 115

Gretzky, Wayne, 16

Griffey, Ken, 113

gunpowder, 149

Guo, Shiqiang, 203

H

Halberstam, David, 69, 138

Hamilton, Philip "Sarge," 106

heroism, 34

hockey, 16, 46

Hogan, Ben, 16

Hong Kong, 40–41

Houston, Sam, 108–109

Houston, University of, 9

Houston, 15, 31, 36, 61, 102–103, 109, 112, 169–170

Houston Chronicle, 139

Houston Rockets, 6, 9–14, 16, 50, 53–54, 61, 74, 80, 84–86, 89, 107, 120–122, 125–129, 153, 163, 184–186, 190, 193–195, 198–199, 207–211
  Championship, 6, 9–10
  Compaq Center, 53–54, 170, 177

THE TAO OF YAO

Draft, 6, 10, 24, 67, 107, 152
San Diego, 24, 102, 128, 134,
    140, 152
The Summit, 9, 16, 53
Hu, Yeshun, 108
Human Immunodeficiency Virus
    (HIV), 172
Hyundai, 59

I
Indiana Pacers, 14, 52, 69, 71,
    149, 212
Indiana State, 72
Indiana, University of, 71, 137,
    148
Inouye, Daniel, 65
internet, 53–54, 61, 173–174
Iron Curtain, 70
Issel, Dan, 7
Iverson, Allen, 23, 130, 144, 175

J
Jackson, Phil, 148–149, 155–157,
    161, 163, 165, 167, 171,
    183, 213
    triangle offense, 156–157
James, LeBron, 4, 208
Jamison, Antawn, 186
Japan, 39, 59
Jenkins, Bruce, 135, 138
Jiang, Zemin, 108
Johnson, Earvin "Magic," 10, 13,
    45, 51–73, 75, 80, 82,
    99, 131, 167, 172, 190, 210,
    212, 214
Johnson, Jack, 57
Johnson, Lyndon, 63

Johnson, Robert, 199
Johnson Jr., Ernie, 85
Jordan, Michael, 3, 10, 44,
    51–53, 75–76, 82, 86, 113,
    155, 159, 167, 172,
    175–176, 184, 199–200

K
Karangwa, Prosper, 188
Karl, George, 188
Kasparov, Gary, 214
Kentucky, University of, 152
Kentucky Fried Chicken (KFC),
    106
Kerlan, Dr. Robert, 96
Key, Francis Scott, 149
Kim, Alice, 59
Kim, Mi-Hyun, 59
King, Billie Jean, 57
King Kong, 161
Kissinger, Henry, 11
Knight, Bobby, 71, 137, 148
Kodak, 210
Korean War, 37
Kukoc, Toni, 47
Kwiatkowski, Andrew, 188

L
Ladies Professional Golf
    Association (LPGA), 59
Lapchick, Joe, 205
Latinos, 58
Lee, Bruce, 65, 154, 163
Lee, Wen Ho, 37
Leonard, John, 147
Li, Jet, 17
Li, Zhangmin, 3, 42

Ling, Lisa, 212–213
Lippmann, Walter, 38
Lithuania, 47
Lloyd, Earl, 58
Lloyd, Scott, 184
Locke, Gary, 65
Los Angeles, 42, 61, 76, 159, 171, 175
Los Angeles Clippers, 43, 164
    San Diego, 6
Los Angeles Dodgers, 57–59
    Brooklyn Dodgers, 57
Los Angeles Lakers, 13, 49, 72, 76, 84, 129–131, 138, 147–148, 152, 159–160, 162–163, 166, 170–172, 174–175, 177, 183–186, 190
    Showtime, 95–96, 152
Los Angeles, University of California (UCLA), 5, 58, 133–135, 138, 190
    Pauley Pavillion, 6
Lott, Trent, 167
Louis, Joe, 57
Louisiana State University (LSU), 141, 160, 164, 167
Loyola Marymount University, 24
Loyola University, Chicago, 14
Luis, Nelson, 54
Lyons, Terry, 50

M
Madden, John, 16
Major League Baseball (MLB), 46, 91

Rookie of the Year, 57, 59
Malone, Karl, 130
Malone, Moses, 10, 80, 142, 152, 170, 182, 184, 207
Mao, Tse-tung, 11, 37, 151
Maravich, Pete, 140–141
Marciulionis, Sarunas, 47
martial arts, 116, 154–155
Martin, Kenyon, 186
Martin, LaRue, 67
Marx, Karl, 39, 200
Maryland, University of, 126
mass media, 15–16, 28, 32, 165–166, 171, 205–207
Matsui, Hideki, 59
McClintock, Dan, 102
McEnroe, John, 117
McGrady, Tracy, 143–144, 175, 193
McHale, Kevin, 7, 139–140
McLeod, John, 25
Mead, Margaret, 1
Memphis Grizzlies, 13
Mengke, Bateer, 74, 203
Messnick, Andrew, 51
Mexico, 39, 58, 108–109
Miami Heat, 55, 123
Michigan, University of, 128
Michigan State, 72, 137
Mikan, George, 182
Milwaukee Bucks, 78, 96, 130, 186, 188
Mineta, Norm, 65
Minnesota, University of, 139
Minnesota Timberwolves, 83, 131, 140, 189–190
Mitchell, Stephen, 113, 115,

178–179

Mobley, Cuttino, 129, 152–153, 211

Monroe, Earl, 155

Montana, Joe, 113

moon, 22–23, 51

Mourning, Alonzo, 69, 130, 182

Movies, *see Films*

Moyers, Bill, 62–63

MSNBC, 212

Mumford, Lewis, 69,

Murphy, Calvin, 128–129, 140

Musburger, Brent, 173,

Mutombo, Dikembe, 46, 120, 130

N

Nachbar, Bostjan, 107

Naismith, James, 6, 47

National Basketball Association (NBA), 2–3, 5–6, 8, 12–15, 36–37, 44–48, 58, 66, 69, 73–75, 78–79, 84, 91, 94–97, 109, 111, 118, 123, 125, 130–131, 139, 152, 166–167, 189, 199, 207, 210

All-Defense Team, 44, 119, 130, 192,

All-Rookie Team, 76, 199

All-Star, 9, 44, 71–72, 76, 79, 81, 89, 102, 126, 130, 143, 160, 173–176, 192

Coach of the Year, 144,

draft, 6, 9–11, 24, 45, 48, 67, 70–72, 76, 107, 128, 152, 204,

foreign players, 46–48, 50–52

Hall of Fame, 6, 13, 75, 89, 122, 128, 193, 205, 211,

MVP, 2, 6, 13, 44, 72, 81, 96, 128, 130, 170, 174, 182,

Rookie of the Month, 14,

Rookie of the Year, 44, 48, 71, 126, 160, 176, 199

Sixth Man, 6,

Top 50 Players, 13, 75, 82, 115, 139, 182, 193

World Championship, 2, 6, 10, 13, 44, 71, 89, 96, 98, 131, 140, 148, 155, 160, 174, 186, 190,

National Collegiate Athletic Association (NCAA), 5, 10, 71–73, 89, 133, 135, 141, 190

National Football League (NFL), 46

National Geographic Explorer, 212

National Hocket League (NHL), 46

National Invitational Tournament (NIT), 135

Navratilova, Martina, 57

Nelson, Don, 25, 43, 47

Nelson, Donn, 43, 47

New Jersey Nets, 120, 132

New York, 2, 45, 51, 61, 63, 97, 205

New York Jets, 117

New York Knicks, 25, 60, 122, 148, 155, 193

New York Mets, 117

New York Times, 51, 147, 171

New York Yankees, 59, 117
Newcombe, Don, 57
Newell, Big Man Camp,
    137–138, 186
Newell, Pete, 3, 135–141, 159,
    183–184, 186–187
Niagara College, 128
Nicaragua, 121
Nietzsche, Frederick, 161
Nigeria, 9
Nike, 3–4, 44, 93, 204
Nixon, Richard, 11
Nomo, Hideo, 59
Nowitzki, Dirk, 48–49, 51, 78,
    129, 183, 192, 209

O
Olajuwon, Hakeem "The Dream,"
    9–10, 46, 84, 88, 119, 126,
    167, 170, 177, 180, 186,
    190–193, 207
Olympics, 43, 57, 116–117
  1956, 115
  1960, 135
  1964, 8
  1984, 44
  1988, 76
  1992, 44, 47, 75, 82
  1996, 76, 160, 82
  2000, 5–6, 8, 83, 153
  2008, 39
O'Neal, Shaquille, 3, 8, 13–14,
    52, 65, 76, 84, 88, 106, 129,
    156, 160–178, 183–184,
    186, 193, 199, 207,
    209–210
  Shaq-Fu, 160,

O'Neal, Jermaine, 52
Oregon, University of, 200
Orlando Magic, 143, 160, 175,
    184, 193, 198
Owens, Jesse, 57
Owens, Terrell, 117

P
Pak, Se Ri, 59
Parish, Robert, 182
Park, Alice, 59
Park, Chan Ho, 59
Park, Grace, 59
Payton, Gary, 130
Pelé, 16
People's Republic of China
    (PRC), 2, 11, 37, 39–41, 43,
    46
Pepsi, Gatorade, 203, 210
Pepsi, 203, 210
Petrovic, Drazen, 47
Philadelphia 76ers, 8, 23, 80, 88,
    100, 144, 184
phoenix, 100
Phoenix Suns, 80, 152, 198–199,
    209
Piazza, Mike, 117
Piccolo, Brian, 125
Pine, Colin, 104–105, 109–112
Pippen, Scottie, 155, 186
Pitino, Rick, 25
Pittsburgh Pirates, 121
Polo, Marco, 11,
Portland Trail Blazers, 6–7, 24,
    48, 50, 67, 69–70, 98, 190
Postolos, George, 53
Presley, Elvis, 89, 200

Public Broadcasting System
(PBS), 62

R
Ramsey, Jack, 69
Ratliff, Theo, 153
Reebok, 210
Reed, Willis, 155, 182
religion, 39, 200
Rhoads, Terry, 4, 204
Rice, Glen, 72, 129
Rice University, 109
Rickey, Branch, 57
Riley, Pat, 10, 25, 45, 123, 132,
134, 147, 151–152
Rivers, Glenn "Doc," 193
Robertson, Oscar, 58, 71, 135,
186
Robinson, David, 48, 50, 74, 167
Robinson, Jackie, 57–58, 60
Rock, Chris, 197
Rose, Pete, 117
Rowell, Robert, 52–53
Rupp, Adolph, 152
Russell, Bill, 2, 17, 31, 58, 83,
115, 118, 130, 148, 167,
177–178, 182

S
Sabonis, Arvydas, 47–49, 70–71,
214
Sacramento Kings, 24, 76–77,
114, 127, 132
Cincinnati Royals, 58
Kansas City Kings, 24
Salon.com, 161
Sampson, Ralph, 6, 183–185

San Antonio Spurs, 14, 74, 113,
130
San Francisco, 42, 52, 55–56, 61,
206
San Francisco 49ers, 117
San Francisco, University of
(USF), 28, 135, 137
Sanders, Bill, 202, 204
Sasser, James, 60
Saunders, Flip, 139–140,
189–190
Sayers, Gayle, 125
Schaap, Dick, 113
Scott, Byron, 131–132
Seattle Mariners, 59
Seattle Supersonics, 96
Sever Acute Respiratory
Syndrome (SARS), 23, 39,
210
Shanghai, Shanghai Sports
College, 4
Shanghai, 1, 41–42, 45, 103, 109,
124–125, 202
Shanghai Morning Post, 12
Shanghai Sharks, Luwan Stadium,
124
Shanghai Sharks, 3–4, 11–12, 42,
102, 119, 124, 135, 213
Shu Kingdom, 151
Silver, Liz, 204
Simmons, Bill, 3, 88, 142–143,
192, 207
sleeping, 98–99
Smith, Kenny, 48, 83–86
Smith, Larry, 198
soccer, 16, 46–47, 186
Sorenstam, Annika, 57

South Korea, 59, 73
Soviet Union, *see USSR*
Spain, 82, 108
Sporting News, 196, 199
Sports Illustrated, 52, 197–200, 202
sportsmanship, 117
Star Wars, 154
Stern, David, 45–46, 50–51, 67
Stockton, John, 10, 71
Stone, Oliver, 149
Stoudemire, Amare, 176, 198–199
Stoudemire, Damon, 48
Sudan, 46
sun, 22–24
Sunday Herald, UK, 213
Suzuki, Ichiro, 59

T

Tai chi, 154, 156, 179, 187
Taiwan, 37, 151
Tang, Irwin, 165, 171
Tao Te Ching, 29, 113, 212–213
Taoism, 17, 113, 149, 154, 157, 188
    Tao, 19–21, 25, 27, 115, 124–125, 142, 155–156, 215
    wei wu wei, 30–31, 178–179
Taylor, Maurice, 94
television, 6, 25, 43, 51–54, 62, 74, 82–83, 85, 117, 164, 172, 199, 210, 212
tennis, 16, 57, 117, 122
Texas, 93, 100, 102, 108–109
Texas A & M, 108

Thanksgiving, 105, 111
The Art of War, 148–149
Thomas, Isiah, 71
Thomaselli, Rich, 52
Thompson, John, 130–131
Thompson, Mychal, 190
Thoreau, Henry David, 93, 208
Thorpe, Jim, 57
Three Gorges Dam, 42
Thurmond, Nate, 182
Tiananmen Square, 39, 41
Tibet, 39
Tilden, Bill, 57
Time Magazine, 187, 198
Tomjanovich, Rudy, 5, 8–10, 25, 53, 67, 74–75, 79, 86–89, 94, 99, 101–102, 107, 111, 120–121, 128, 140–141, 144–145, 157, 159, 183, 192, 198, 209, 211
Toronto Raptors, 10, 68, 122
Troyer, Vern, 200
Turner Network Television (TNT), 25, 83, 85–86187, 195, 197, 200, 205, 207, 213, 215
Twain, Mark, 18
Tzu, Lao, 1, 19–21, 24–27, 29–33, 35–36, 45, 55, 67, 80, 90–91, 95, 98, 100, 106, 113, 118, 120, 123, 125, 132, 140, 147, 150, 153, 156, 161, 168–169, 172, 177–178, 181
Tzu, Sun, 147, 149–151, 153–154, 156, 159, 161, 164, 165, 168–169, 173, 177

U

United States Golf Association (USGA), 60
Unseld, Wes, 182
United States (US), 2, 11, 36–39, 63–64, 105–106, 165
 1954 Brown v. Board of Education, 60
 1964 Civil Rights Act, 60
 1965 Voting Rights Act, 60
 Declaration of Independence, 55
 FBI, 37
 racism, 58, 166
 trade, 39
 Transcontinental Railroad, 63
USA Today, 121
USSR,
 glasnost, 70
 Iron Curtain, 70
 perestroika, 70
Utah Jazz, 130

V

Valenzuela, Fernando, 59
Van Gundy, Bill, 123
Van Gundy, Jeff, 25, 79, 86, 123, 148, 193–194, 210–211
Van Gundy, Stan, 123
Vandeweghe, Kiki, 138, 183
VISA, 202, 204
Vitale, Dick, 67

W

Wallace, Ben, 119, 141–142
Walton, Bill, 5–8, 69, 80–81, 89, 98–99, 112, 119, 123–124, 134, 167, 184, 186, 190, 192, 214
Wang, Bob, 61
Wang, L. Ling-chi, 62
Wang, Qun, 42
Wang, Zhi Zhi, 43, 47, 50, 74, 164
Warring States period, 27, 215
Washington, Kermit, 101, 137–139
Washington Post, 45, 182
Washington Wizards, 86, 146, 180
water, 21, 26, 163, 188
West, Jerry, 13, 76, 135, 138–139, 152, 189
Wie, Michelle, 60
Wilkens, Lenny, 122
Williams, Frank, 209
Williams, Jay, 67
Williams, Pat, 184
Williams, Serena, 16, 199
Wimbledon, 117
Wooden, John, 5, 98–99, 116, 122, 133–136, 190
Woods, Tiger, 59, 197, 199
World Trade Organization (WTO), 39

X

xenophobia, 48, 62–63
Xin Min Evening News, 42
Xinhua News Agency, 203

Y

Yan, Xiao Xian, 42
Yang, 19–20, 163

Yangtze River, 42, 151
Yanjing Beer, 54
Yao, Zhi Yuan, 103
Yao Ming Fan Club, 61
Yaomingmania.com, 61
Ye, Li, 101
Yin, 19–20, 163
Yugoslavia, 76, 143
    Belgrade, 37

Croatia, 47
Serbia, 47

Z
Zaire, 46
Zhai, May, 203
Zhu, Geliang, 151
Zinn, Howard, 57
Zweig, Paul, 34

THE TAO OF YAO

Oliver Chin has been a lifelong basketball fan, weekend warrior, and an aficionado of regional sports rivalries as he has lived in Los Angeles, Boston, New York, and San Francisco. Graduating from Harvard University with a degree in Social Studies, he concentrated in Popular Culture and Mass Media with a *magna cum laude* senior thesis *Just Do It: Sports Advertising and the American Dream*. A columnist on entertainment and media trends, he recently wrote and illustrated the acclaimed graphic novel *Nine of One: A Window to the World*. Currently he resides with his wife Amy and son Lucas in San Francisco, CA.

Also by Oliver Chin

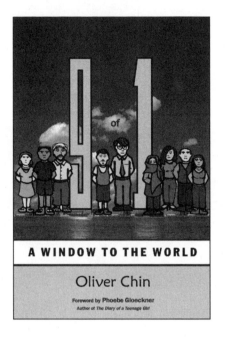

Nine of One: A Window to the World

$12.95 US, ISBN: 1-58394-072-3, www.9of1.com

"[Chin is] using comics to educate readers and examine the world around us.... **Nine of One** is intended to open readers to a spectrum of opinions from the rainbow that is America at its best.... [It] is notable for its lofty societal aspirations and for going where few American comics have gone."

—*Comics Buyer's Guide*

"Reviewer's Choice:

Especially recommended as supplemental reading for students of contemporary international studies arising from the current 'war on terrorism', **Nine of One: A Window To The World** is a graphic novel style history about a teacher who assigns nine students to interview a variety of people, and in the process they learn an amazing selection of diverse perspectives and ways understanding the world about them. Educational, fascinating, even-handedly informative, and suitable for all readers of ages and backgrounds, this contemplative read accessibly explores the many ways in which humans live their lives in an upbeat and engrossing manner."

—*Midwest Book Review*

"Chin provides students with a wide variety of viewpoints on world affairs, giving some important historical background ... this is a commendable effort: by putting these views in the mouths of ordinary people, Chin brings large issues into personal focus and provides a useful teaching tool. Recommended for schools and for young adult collections."

—*Library Journal*

"Despite what [others] may have to say on the matter, books like **Nine of One** and other forms of balanced, intelligent examination of the after-effects of 9-11 are still to be found in America."

—TheFourthRail.com